More Praise for *Rebuilding Trust in the Workplace*

"*The* definitive book on sustaining trust in your organization. Dennis and Michelle Reina have created a practical manual for understanding, building, and rebuilding trust in working relationships."

—**Paul Rosner, Chief Information Officer, Energy Coal, BHP Billiton, Sydney, Australia**

"The Reinas' true-to-life stories inspired me to reframe broken trust and arrive in a place of renewed energy and understanding."

—**Peggy Niemer, Corporate Vice President, Human Resources, Children's Hospital and Health System**

"Dennis and Michelle demonstrate their profound understanding of the human spirit and human frailties—and their ability to step back and observe the strengths that can come from both. I believe this book is for everyone in relationships everywhere, not just those in the workplace."

—**Stephen H. Rhinesmith, PhD, coauthor of *Head, Heart, and Guts***

"Michelle and Dennis Reina are at the forefront of helping leaders understand the importance of trust in building high performance organizations. *Rebuilding Trust in the Workplace* presents actionable concepts that leaders can put to immediate use in rebuilding trust in relationships in the workplace as well as at home."

—**Deborah Garrett, Vice President, Human Resources, Intuit**

"The principles in this book have had an important and valuable influence on how members of our team talk to each other, how we treat each other, and how we expect to be treated by others. The Reinas' work has given us a gift that allowed us to move forward. We found a path to becoming better individuals and teammates."

—**David J. Whaley, Vice President, Development and Alumni Relations, Norwich University**

"As organizations become more diverse, trust emerges as a critical prerequisite for the conversations necessary to align different world views in support of a common mission and vision. *Rebuilding Trust in the Workplace* breaks this seemingly complex issue into kaizen-like steps that can help employees, supervisors, and leaders effectively manage and best leverage a multicultural workforce."

—**Harry R. Gibbs, MD, Chief Diversity Officer, MD Anderson Cancer Center, Houston**

"Given that trust is fragile—it can be built and broken—knowing how to rebuild trust is essential. *Rebuilding Trust in the Workplace* offers practical advice and guidance for how to build and bolster trust. And effective leaders know that trust is the foundation for the kind of engagement that drives high quality, sustainable results."

—Sue Hoffman, Program Manager, Talent Acquisition, 3M

"As a multidimensional nonprofit agency, we see the demand for our services at an all-time high. With pressure on staff and stress in relationships peaking, I will use this book daily in my work with managers and our teams. I know its advice will produce great results."

—Jill C. Dagilis Executive Director, Worcester Community Action Council

"By applying the Reinas' proven methods and tools for rebuilding trust, you will come to learn more about yourself and others. You will also learn how to create and sustain the strong relationships that are necessary to navigate today's complex environment. Read this practical, easy-to-read book and turn the elusive trust we all seek into reality!"

—Kate Beatty, Director, Global Portfolio Management, Center for Creative Leadership

"This book speaks to managers as imperfect beings—the reality is that in our work organizations, we have the potential to inadvertently be on both sides of a complex trust issue, feeling betrayed and instigating betrayal. *Rebuilding Trust in the Workplace* not only explains this paradox but also shows how to reflect internally and then take action."

—Thom Johnston, President, New England School of Communications

"Workplace trust is at an all-time low. Fortunately there is help within the pages of *Rebuilding Trust in the Workplace*. Dennis and Michelle Reina adeptly describe the issues underpinning the loss of trust while giving readers ways to reframe their thinking. The authors also provide pragmatic steps that can be put to use immediately to rebuild trust among coworkers."

—Jon Peters, President, The Institute for Management Studies

"There has never been a greater sense of the loss of trust in the religious community than there is today. Every congregational member or clergy leader has found himself or herself at one or more of the vantage points of betrayal outlined in *Rebuilding Trust in the Workplace,* whether we realize it or not, for broken trust is all around us. Thank goodness we now have a road map in the form of this approachable, compassionate book."

—Rev. Phill Martin, CAE, CCA, Deputy CEO, National Association of Church Business Administration

"*Rebuilding Trust in the Workplace* is equally powerful in both one-on-one relationships and group settings. A central theme in the book involves taking responsibility, whether you are the betrayer or the victim, in order to move forward in the healing process. The book offers practical yet thought-provoking advice and provides an excellent framework for rebuilding trust."
—**Barbara Kimmel, Executive Director, Trust Across America**

"*Rebuilding Trust in the Workplace* is a very useful guide that provides an easy-to-understand process, a helpful framework, a variety of real-world examples, useful tips, and memorable quotations. I appreciated the well-rounded perspective that addresses both the betrayed and betrayer, invokes both compassion and courage, and details how to give to yourself and others."
—**Simon Hayward, Managing Partner, Cirrus, Cheshire, UK**

"This book will help individuals heal their relationships with intention and courage. It provides a proven path to reclaim trust and restore the relationships that underpin satisfaction, performance, and achievement at work."
—**Leslie Yerkes, President, Catalyst Consulting Group, Inc.; and adjunct faculty member, Case Western Reserve University; and author of *Fun Works* and *They Just Don't Get It!***

"As a leader, I'm always looking for tools that will help supervisors, whether at the executive level or on the front lines, be the best managers they can be. In this book, I found such a tool. Its practical model and real-life stories make it accessible and effective for anyone tackling the challenge of broken trust."
—**Ted A. Mayer, Executive Director, Harvard University Hospitality and Dining Services**

"Rebuilding trust should be a competency required of all leaders and all individual contributors across all organizations. Dennis and Michelle Reina tell us how to hone the skills that will prepare us to repair damaged relationships. All who read *Rebuilding Trust in the Workplace* will come away with a deeper understanding of themselves and a greater appreciation of others."
—**Beverly Kaye, Founder and CEO, Career Systems International, and coauthor of *Love 'Em or Lose 'Em***

"Do you have a hard time winning back the hearts of your employees? Has your team become paranoid? Do you wonder what to do and where to start? If so, your top priority should be reading *Rebuilding Trust in the Workplace*. You'll find valuable insights to spot trust-breakers and practical tips to shepherd the healing process."
—**Philippe Masson, Founding Partner and President, MyDevelopment.Pro, Paris, France**

"Trust is a fragile thing—easy to break and hard to repair—but rebuilding trust is a job you cannot ignore if you want a thriving workplace. Don't miss this book. The trust you rebuild may be in yourself."
—John Kador, author of *Effective Apology*

"Dennis and Michelle Reina walk the reader through a process that can lead beyond personal feelings and reactions to effective resolution. This book addresses a very important missing link in most companies' handling of human resource issues!"
—Randy Spencer, Vice President for Residential Services, Presbyterian Children's Homes & Services

"We all know that people, performance, and profits suffer when trust is broken. Dennis and Michelle Reina provide step-by-step guidance for healing personally and organizationally. Follow their sage advice to re-establish leadership credibility and create a positive emotional environment in your organization."
—Diana Whitney, PhD, President, Corporation for Positive Change, and author of Appreciative Leadership

"Trust is at the core of the best schools I have worked in and visited, and it is evident in each school's top educators and administrators. Yet it's hard to imagine a group of organizations more in need of trust rebuilding than our public schools. I hope all schools tap into this book, for Dennis and Michelle provide clear, proven steps on strengthening the trustful relationships that are essential among students, teachers, parents, and administrators."
—Heidi Berlyak, Owner, LearningReviews.com

"*Rebuilding Trust in the Workplace* is likely to be one of the most important books on workplace relationships you will ever read. Full of compelling and moving real-life examples, it speaks directly to you, draws you in, and makes you feel part of the story. There were times, in fact, when I thought I was the person they were writing about. Dennis and Michelle Reina are exceptional coaches who walk you through a proven process. From the first page to the last, you will find useful things you can do immediately to heal a broken relationship and steer it back to one that's renewing and productive. Do yourself a big favor and buy this book now, read it tonight, and put it to use tomorrow. You'll thank yourself and so will those you work with."
—Jim Kouzes, Dean's Executive Professor of Leadership, Leavey School of Business, Santa Clara University and coauthor of *The Leadership Challenge* and *The Truth About Leadership*

REBUILDING TRUST IN THE WORKPLACE

REBUILDING TRUST IN THE WORKPLACE

Seven Steps to Renew Confidence, Commitment, and Energy

Dennis Reina and Michelle Reina

Berrett–Koehler Publishers, Inc.
San Francisco
a BK Business book

Berrett-Koehler Publishers, Inc.
235 Montgomery Street, Suite 650
San Francisco, CA 94104-2916
Tel: (415) 288-0260   Fax: (415) 362-2512   www.bkconnection.com

Ordering Information

Quantity sales. Special discounts are available on quantity purchases by corporations, associations, and others. For details, contact the "Special Sales Department" at the Berrett-Koehler address above.

Individual sales. Berrett-Koehler publications are available through most bookstores. They can also be ordered directly from Berrett-Koehler: Tel: (800) 929-2929; Fax: (802) 864-7626; www.bkconnection.com

Orders for college textbook/course adoption use. Please contact Berrett-Koehler: Tel: (800) 929-2929; Fax: (802) 864-7626.

Orders by U.S. trade bookstores and wholesalers. Please contact Ingram Publisher Services, Tel: (800) 509-4887; Fax: (800) 838-1149; E-mail: customer.service@ingrampublisherservices.com; or visit www.ingrampublisherservices.com/Ordering for details about electronic ordering.

Berrett-Koehler and the BK logo are registered trademarks of Berrett-Koehler Publishers, Inc.

Printed in the United States of America

Berrett-Koehler books are printed on long-lasting acid-free paper. When it is available, we choose paper that has been manufactured by environmentally responsible processes. These may include using trees grown in sustainable forests, incorporating recycled paper, minimizing chlorine in bleaching, or recycling the energy produced at the paper mill.

Library of Congress Cataloging-in-Publication Data

Reina, Dennis S., 1950-
 Rebuilding trust in the workplace : seven steps to renew confidence, commitment, and
  energy / Dennis Reina and Michelle Reina.
   p. cm.
  Includes bibliographical references and index.
  ISBN 978-1-60509-372-7 (alk. paper)
  1. Organizational behavior. 2. Trust. 3. Interpersonal relations. 4. Work environment.
  5. Organizational effectiveness. 6. Psychology, Industrial. I. Reina, Michelle L., 1958-
  II. Title.
  HD58.7.R4387 2010
  658.3'145--dc22   2010031469

First Edition
15 14 13 12 11 10   10 9 8 7 6 5 4 3 2 1

Interior design and project management by Jonathan Peck, Dovetail Publishing Services.
Cover design by pemastudio; Cover photo © masashi sakajiri/iStockPhoto

In loving memory of Michelle's father,

Jack R. Chagnon, 1930–2009

Through his courage and compassion,
he taught us the gift of forgiveness, healing,
and renewal.

Contents

Preface

If you feel that trust within your workplace has been broken, you are not alone. It doesn't mean that you work with "bad" people or that you are naïve. Behaviors that break trust are experienced daily in workplaces around the world. Chances are you've breached someone else's trust at work without even realizing it.

Broken trust is simply the natural outcome of people interacting with one another. There are times when trust is built, and other times when trust is destroyed, or, more often, gradually eroded by a series of small, unintentional breaches. Yet trust can and will be rebuilt if you commit to taking courageous and compassionate steps.

How do you know if you're experiencing broken trust? You may:

- Be less engaged, less committed, and more skeptical
- Resist volunteering for assignments
- Find yourself feeling isolated at work
- Hear that people are talking about you behind your back
- Have a nagging feeling of discomfort about something you've said or done
- See that others are anxious at work and feel awkward in not knowing how to respond
- Feel caught in the middle of office politics or co-workers' interpersonal conflicts
- Notice that you are just going through the motions at work
- Miss work or often arrive late

These feelings and reactions are normal. We all experience the breach of trust in our relationships, both at work and at home. But not everyone is motivated to work through those feelings and find alternative ways to react. The very fact that you sit with this book in your hands shows that you value connected relationships that honor people for who they are and for what they bring to the workplace and to one another.

This book is for you, no matter where you are with trust at work. You may have experienced the loss of trust as a result of what others have done to you. You may be struggling with the realization that you have inadvertently broken trust, letting others down and causing them pain. You may be looking for direction to help others who are in pain due to patterns of distrust around them. Or, perhaps, you're relishing the positive energy and performance that comes from knowing that you trust your colleagues and they trust you, and you're inspired to learn how to maintain that flow. You may simply be interested in a general exploration of rebuilding trust so that you can help sustain effective relationships.

In the twenty years that we've been researching trust in the workplace, we have provided training programs and consulting services to hundreds of organizations large and small, public and private, for- and not-for profit, around the world. While many people have attempted to describe trust, we have gone further to develop thoroughly tested, statistically sound instruments to *measure* trust; these instruments give voice to that which people experience and feel, and provide actionable data. In 1999, we wrote a book called *Trust and Betrayal in the Workplace: Building Effective Relationships in Your Organization*; we revised and expanded it in 2006. In that book, we provided the following comprehensive overview of trust:

- The three specific types of trust and the sixteen concrete behaviors that build them
- People's readiness and willingness to trust themselves and others
- The behaviors that break trust

- The impact of betrayal
- The characteristics that cultivate transformation through trust building
- An introduction to the steps to *rebuild* trust

Time and time again since that book, people have asked us to go deeper into the area of rebuilding trust. *Rebuilding Trust in the Workplace* is an answer to those requests. We wrote this book because you asked us to. In it, we extend an invitation for you and your colleagues to learn how to renew relationships at work. We give you a place to go to understand your own feelings of hurt, disappointment, let-down and pain that come with broken trust, and to understand the pain of others. You will tap into the hope that is embedded in all rela-tionships—hope that can be uncovered through healing. Through an approach that is both constructive and compassionate, you will learn practical, actionable steps for rebuilding trust. You will deepen your understanding of yourself and of your relationships, and you will dis-cover the gifts pain can bring when you choose to heal.

We begin with an introduction about the nature of trust and how it can be destroyed or eroded, and the impact of broken trust. We explore the topic from three vantage points:

- When you've been hurt by others
- When you've hurt someone else
- When you want to help others rebuild trust

We describe the pathway to rebuild trust: The Seven Steps for Healing.[1] Chapters One through Seven walk you through each Step and provide practical advice for each vantage point so that you can apply the lessons to your specific situation. Information at the begin-ning of each chapter is relevant to each of the vantage points. You'll find a recap of the Steps and an overview of the benefits of rebuilding trust in Chapter Eight.

In the chapters, you will find trust tips, reflection questions, and practical how-to exercises to help you put your learning into action, individually and with others, immediately. Because we have discovered that people gain insights from others' experiences, we tell stories—even a few of our own—throughout the book. In the process of helping organizations, we have listened to and coached thousands of people at all levels. Their voices are reflected in these pages. Additionally, we conducted over twenty-five in-depth interviews specifically for this book. We asked these individuals to share their experience moving through the Seven Steps. The resulting material, shared anonymously under fictitious names, provides real-life examples that we hope are useful to you. At the same time, these interviews proved important and healing for the people we spoke to. Many, especially those who came to terms with their role in hurting others, shed tears while they recounted their healing journeys. Through their tears, they discovered insights about relationships that they will carry with them forever.

Like each of these courageous people, by applying the Seven Steps, you'll rebuild trust and renew the confidence, commitment, and energy that were eroded by the loss of trust. You will come to know yourself more deeply. You will want to go to work and you will feel safe to be more fully "who" you are. In that place of safety, you'll give your organization your best thinking, highest intention, full spirit, risk-taking and creativity. And from a place of personal self-discovery, self-trust and authenticity, you will succeed not only professionally, but personally as well.

Dennis and Michelle Reina
April, 2010
Stowe, Vermont

REBUILDING TRUST IN THE WORKPLACE

Betrayal Is Universal

The vulnerability of trust is always present, even in high-trust relationships. Since business is transacted through relationships, it follows that you will experience times at work when trust is broken— sometimes obviously, and sometimes not so obviously. Each and every day, small but hurtful situations accumulate over time into confidence-busting, commitment-breaking, energy-draining patterns consistent with broken trust. People feel hurt, disappointed, let down, and frustrated. The feelings can be as strong as resentment, bitterness, antipathy, and even betrayal.

Betrayal is not our word. It is the word used by the thousands of people we have worked with who have taught us about trust. Betrayal is often viewed as a dark, negative word that triggers painful memories. But when trust has been broken, people often feel betrayed. That is the simple truth. It is also true that every single one of us has been betrayed and has betrayed others. Betrayal is universal. People have been betrayed by bosses, subordinates, co-workers. There is betrayal in families, friendships, neighborhoods, social groups, religious institutions, schools, and universities. The ways trust is broken aren't always immediate or obvious. Let's start by learning more about the forms betrayal takes.

Every single one of us has been betrayed and has betrayed others.

1

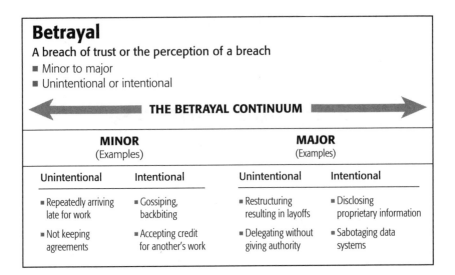

The Betrayal Continuum

Betrayal occurs on a continuum from unintentional to intentional and from minor to major. Intentional betrayal is a self-serving action committed with the purpose of hurting, damaging, or harming another person. Unintentional betrayal is the by-product of a self-serving or careless action that has the same result.

Major betrayals impact you immediately and dramatically at your deepest core. At work, major betrayal is often associated with mismanaged change related to reorganizations, shifts in strategy, mergers, acquisitions, and layoffs. On a more interpersonal level, a major betrayal may occur through a single act, such as violating a confidence or telling a lie. Major intentional betrayals are often the outcomes of fear and self-serving interests and include situations in which people:

- Deliberately fail to honor their commitments
- Knowingly withhold information
- Deceive fellow co-workers
- Sabotage others' work to further their own ends

Major intentional betrayals are hurtful, ill-intended words or actions that break down trusting relationships. As one concerned

Common Workplace Minor Betrayals

- Gossiping or talking about others behind their backs
- Consistently arriving late for meetings
- Not responding to requests made by others
- Hoarding pertinent, job-related information
- Not returning phone calls or answering email requests
- Finger pointing and blaming
- Covering up mistakes
- Discourteous, insensitive, or rude behavior
- Taking credit for others' work

Many unintentional minor betrayals have to do with abdicating responsibility. These are subtle situations in which someone tries to let him or herself off the hook by:

- Telling a white lie
- Not fully disclosing information
- Condoning or not responding to someone else's inappropriate behavior
- Not owning his or her part of problem
- Allowing his or her co-workers or reports to fail when he or she could have stepped in and helped.

employee told us, "It is especially painful when you are stabbed in the back without warning by those closest to you. It knocks you off your feet."

While major betrayals decisively break trust, minor unintentional betrayals that erode trust over time are more pervasive. Take a look at the box for examples of such common behaviors. Our research shows that 90 percent of employees experience these types of betrayal frequently. But instead of dealing directly with these transgressions, people let them go unaddressed. Importantly, however, they do not go unnoticed. The net result of the accumulation of minor betrayals is major: people mentally and emotionally check out. They may wait it out until the economy improves to walk out the door. In the mean-time, they become the "working wounded," those who do as little as they can to get away with, no more, no less. Relationships fall apart and everyone loses.

How you position an experience along the betrayal continuum depends on the degree to which you perceive that the individual was self-serving or careless and the degree of hurt, damage, or pain actu-ally inflicted. For instance, someone accepting credit for someone else's work may be a minor intentional betrayal in one circumstance, but if the person who falsely accepts credit does so knowing that he will gain greatly at the other's expense, it is a major intentional betrayal. We recently worked with a leader who lost a promotional opportunity because a co-worker took full credit for her work. This lost opportunity represented a major betrayal.

» Trust Tip   In order to fully understand trust, we must understand betrayal. Betrayal is a natural part of human relationships. Critical to the health of human relationships is how effectively we deal with and work through betrayal when it happens.

The Impact of Betrayal

No matter its source, betrayal can rock you to your core and strike at the very center of your humanness. When you are vulnerable, your feelings are raw. You may feel sick to your stomach, have frequent headaches, or be more susceptible to illness. You may feel broken. You lose your footing, withdraw, pull back, disengage, and contract. In your contraction, you become hesitant and reluctant to trust oth-ers and yourself. You doubt yourself, question your own trustworthi-ness, and contemplate your sense of belonging. You wonder, who can I trust, who can't I trust? Who can I believe, who can't I believe? Your sense of self and identity flounders. You ask, what did I do to deserve this, who am I, and what do I have to offer?

In short, when you feel betrayed, you lose the *confidence, commitment, and energy* that keep relationships together, fuel your performance, and feed your satisfaction at work. Let's take these one at a time:

Confidence:

"A co-worker is always speaking over me in discussions or when we make group presentations. I try to contribute but I struggle to make myself heard. I hold back my opinions because I feel like my co-workers place no value in what I have to say. **I feel insecure and lack confidence in my opinions and my value to the company.**"

When someone has betrayed you, you lose confidence in that person. If you feel betrayed by your company, you lose confidence in your leadership and sometimes in your colleagues. Over time, with repeated occurrences, you lose confidence in yourself. You begin to question and doubt your competence and your judgment of others. You then are no longer willing to take risks or put in extra effort.

Commitment

"Everyone on our team is constantly forwarding their own interests and pushing hidden agendas. I guess it's probably not the best way to work, but experience has taught me that this is the only way to get what I want. If I stop looking out for myself, someone around me will take advantage of it, and I won't be able to obtain the resources I need to do my work. I'm sorry, but at this point, I have to focus on looking out for myself, because no one else will. **I feel alienated, isolated, and forced to act in a manner against my core values.**"

When someone betrays you, you question your commitment to that relationship. When that relationship is at work, the lack of commitment seeps into your commitment to your team, organization, and career. You simply don't care anymore about the organization's mission, your team's goals, or maybe even about your customers or other constituents you serve. You're ready to leave whenever you get a better offer. You may even be aware of losing connection and commitment to your own values; in other words, you begin to betray *yourself* as well.

Energy

*"Every time I write something, my boss completely rewrites it. I don't understand why he even has me write it in the first place. At this point, I don't even make an effort when drafting up a document, because I know he's going to change the entire thing anyway. It is the most annoying behavior I have ever experienced in the workplace, but there is nothing I can do about it because he's my boss. **I feel devalued and unable to make meaningful contribution. I'm just going through the motions and am so tired when I get home.**"*

Betrayal is energy-depleting and trust is energy-producing. Trust begets trust, and betrayal begets betrayal. When you feel betrayed, it's natural to want to betray the other person back. Betrayal is energy-depleting because you spend what energy you do have plotting negative moves or retreating into a survival mode focused on self-preservation. You become distracted from your job and distanced from your colleagues. You lose sight of what used to motivate you, so work becomes a chore that wears you down.

Betrayals large and small heighten your awareness of trust-related issues and bring you an opportunity for self-discovery and renewal. Pursuing that opportunity is a choice you make consciously. You can choose to remain depleted, without confidence, commitment, or energy or you can choose to renew by being curious and open to learning, growing, and becoming self-aware.

Betrayal: A Gift and a Teacher

"Every failure, obstacle, or hardship is an opportunity in disguise. Success in many cases is failure turned inside out."

—Mary Kay Ash
American businessperson

We know it's hard to choose the path of renewal. When you have been betrayed, you often feel helpless and hopeless. You experience doubt and confusion, question your self-worth and your sense of belonging, and are in pain. You may feel as though you have no control over what was "done to you."

When you remain angry, bitter, or resentful and assume the posture of a victim, you lock into a focus on others' actions. You become consumed in what "they did to you," and allow their actions to eat away at your spirit. Over time your resentment grows and self-pity sets in. You may even choose to betray intentionally in return because "they deserve it." Others experience you as arrogant, self-serving, and irresponsible. You are not a person others want to be around or work with.

Alternatively, you may choose to embrace the pain of betrayal. This choice takes you on a journey of healing and renewal. On this journey, you replace anger and bitterness with compassion. Through compassion, you seek to understand your pain and to work through it to heal and to deepen your understanding of your relationships with yourself and with others. You extend the benefit of the doubt and are willing to hear alternate perspectives. You are curious about insights that may come. With courage, you may even ask yourself if you may have contributed in some way to what occurred.

Through healing, you become:

- More self-aware

- More deeply compassionate

- More self-confident

- Open to learn more about life, people, and relationships

You become a person others want to work with because they know they will have permission to be human when they are around you.

When you deny yourself the opportunity to heal from your pain, you betray yourself. You erode your life force. You rob yourself of insights, lessons, your restored capacity for trust, and potential future opportunities. You rob yourself of yourself. When you choose to embrace your pain and work through it, you regain your wholeness. As a participant said during one of our Trust Building[1] programs, "I am grateful for my experiences of betrayal because of how they contributed to the person I am today. They led me to the relationships I hold most precious and to the place I am in my life."

> *"I am grateful for my experiences of betrayal because of how they contributed to the person I am today."*

In this way, betrayal can be a teacher. When you heal and renew, you transform yourself, your relationships, your organizations, and the world around you.

The Three Vantage Points

You can learn from betrayal, whether you have been betrayed, have betrayed someone else, or want to help others work through betrayal. In this book, we provide information relevant to all vantage points at the beginning of each chapter, and then we give information and advice that is specific to each of these vantage points. Because human relationships are systems, it is unlikely that you will ever fall into just one of these categories. If you are honest with yourself when someone has breached your trust, you will often find that you *also* betrayed that person or yourself. And when you become cognizant of your behavior that betrayed another, you may also discover that you were reacting to having been betrayed by that person, or by someone else entirely. Often, we find that people engage in trust-breaking behavior at work when they have been betrayed at home. Betrayal, as we've said, begets betrayal.

Because broken trust is so pervasive in the workplace, it is likely that you see it around you even if you don't feel directly involved in it. We are often asked by caring people who are concerned about other individuals or the overall work environment what they can do to help others rebuild trust. We applaud the intentions and courage of these people. If you are one of them, we first point you to the material about what to do when you feel betrayed. Why? Because you cannot be an instrument for healing and rebuilding trust if you are currently troubled by (or suffering from) unresolved pain yourself. It's likely that as you help others, your own feelings will surface. Those feelings may be related to what you see in the workplace, or they may be feelings you carry from home or even from your childhood. Be prepared to go on your own journey as you set out to accompany others on theirs. Others have to see you as trustworthy before they will open up to you and be willing to receive your help.

The Seven Steps for Healing

"The man who does things makes mistakes, but he never makes the biggest mistake of all—doing nothing."

—Benjamin Franklin
Statesman, scientist, and one of
America's founding fathers

Whether you are feeling betrayed, coming to terms with having betrayed another, or simply trying to help, the Seven Steps for Healing[2] will provide a process to achieve renewal.

The Seven Steps for Healing model is universal. It emerged out of Dennis's experience with some of the most basic sources of betrayal: broken promises, dishonesty, and abandonment. He found value in understanding the reasons bad things happened, in integrating the lessons to be learned, in forgiving himself and his betrayer, and in letting go and moving on.

My world came crashing down. I came back from a four-day doctorate research session and discovered that my wife had been having an affair with a co-worker for six months. I was stunned, confused, and disoriented. I was angry and upset. But most of all, I questioned myself: How could I not have noticed?

I loved my wife and our two little boys. For the year and a half after discovering the affair, I did whatever I could to hold the marriage togeth-

er. I went to counseling to work through my issues and the pain of my failing marriage, but my wife was not willing to join me in this effort.

We worked out an amicable divorce agreement and were awarded joint custody of our boys. While I had my boys on alternating weekends, some holidays and vacations, I lost the life with them that I had cherished.

A very painful part of the early years after the divorce were my long and sad rides home after dropping the boys off at the end of their weekends with me. I cried so hard, I often had to pull over to the side of the road because I couldn't see straight to drive.

The Seven Steps for Healing

1. Observe and acknowledge what happened
Observe the situation to become aware of what happened, and then fully acknowledge the impact on you, others, and your relationships. When you are betrayed, you often experience the impact as a loss: the loss of what was or the loss of what could have been. For healing to take place, you need to acknowledge that loss.

2. Allow feelings to surface
Express your feelings, whether they are anger, disappointment, hurt, sadness, fear, guilt, or confusion. Give yourself permission to feel upset. Find appropriate ways to release your emotions and give voice to your pain. Allowing your feelings to surface brings about a "release" that allows you to begin to work through your hurt and supports the healing process.

3. Get and give support
Identify support that will help you to recognize where you are stuck or struggling. Support helps you to move from blaming to problem solving. It helps you to move from being "the victim" to taking responsibility for yourself, your job, and your life so that you grow from the experience. You can find support within yourself or from other people.

4. Reframe the experience
Use your hurt and pain as stepping stones for healing. Consider the bigger picture, and what might have been going on for the other person involved and for you. Examine the choices and opportunities you now have. Find the purpose of this event in your life and tease out what you can learn about yourself, others, and relationships.

This intense pain continued for quite some time before subsiding. What I was grieving was the loss of my daily life with my sons—the loss of what could have been, but now would never be. I missed tucking the boys into bed every night, rubbing their backs as they dozed off to sleep. I missed making them breakfast and putting them on the school bus.

In my grieving, I needed to allow my feelings to surface, to release my anger, my hurt, and my deep pain. And I did, again and again.

While living this chapter of my life was a nightmare, years later I was able to see its enormously redeeming value. A powerful lesson for

5. Take responsibility

Courageously look at what part you may have played in what happened. You are not responsible for what was done to you, but you are responsible for how you chose to respond. Consider what you could have done differently, what actions you can take now to change the situation, and the gains you make by taking responsibility.

6. Forgive yourself and others

Compassionately ask what needs to happen for forgiveness to take place. Reflect on how this betrayal occurred. Forgiveness does not mean excusing the offending behavior but rather observing how the betrayal has affected you and others. Consider again your feelings surrounding the betrayal, and decide to release yourself from the burden of carrying those feelings.

7. Let go and move on

Ask what needs to be said or done to put this experience behind you. You do not forget the betrayal or fail to protect yourself from further betrayals. There is a difference between remembering and "hanging on," and remembering so as to help yourself and others by drawing on the lessons learned. Stronger and more self-aware than you were before the trust was broken, you look forward rather than backward. You choose to act differently as you integrate and celebrate your learning.

me was that while I felt victimized, I certainly did not need to remain a
victim. I chose to work through my pain and learned a lot about myself.
I became more sensitive to others in pain, and how I could help them.

Through my healing, I was eventually led to my future wife and
business partner, Michelle. Together, we developed the work that we do
today. And my healing gave birth to the framework of these Seven
Steps for Healing.

The other basis for the Seven Steps for Healing model is the extensive research on the grieving process. Experiencing a betrayal has much in common with experiencing a death. There is a sense of loss. Healing after a betrayal, as after a death, requires us to move through a series of emotions. In her examination of death and dying, Elisabeth Kübler-Ross defined the steps of the grieving process as shock, anger, denial, rationalization, depression, and acceptance.[3] Our Seven Steps for Healing model (see box and figure) tells you how to take action to work through the feelings Kübler-Ross observed. These Steps show a manageable path to help you acknowledge and move through your hurt, with support, to reframe your experience, take responsibility, let go, and move on. Through the Seven Steps you will learn the lessons that betrayal has to teach you about relationships, life, and yourself.

Healing is a process that can't be short-circuited. The effects of broken trust won't go away on their own volition; you have to work through the process of healing. We have all been victims and been betrayed, we have all been perpetrators and betrayed others, and we all have a general desire to help others. No matter where you start, the Seven Steps for Healing are intended to serve as a framework to help you work through the painful feelings of betrayal toward rebuilding the trust that will restore your confidence and commitment and reignite your energy.

Each of the Seven Steps represents a phase of the healing process. Although they are numbered sequentially, people do not necessarily work through them in a linear fashion. You may be experienc-

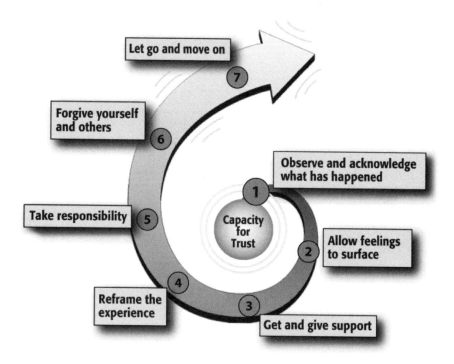

ing multiple Steps at the same time; it is very common to work on observation and acknowledgment (Step One) at the same time as you are allowing your feelings to surface (Step Two) and seeking support (Step Three). Only the starting point, awareness (Step One), is fixed. You may complete one Step and move to the next, only to re-experience aspects of the earlier Step. Feelings come in waves; there are highs and lows, ebbs and flows. All of that is movement toward healing.

> *"There is no comparison between that which is lost by not succeeding and that which is lost by not trying."*
>
> —Francis Bacon
> British statesman and philosopher

1

Observe
and Acknowledge
What Happened

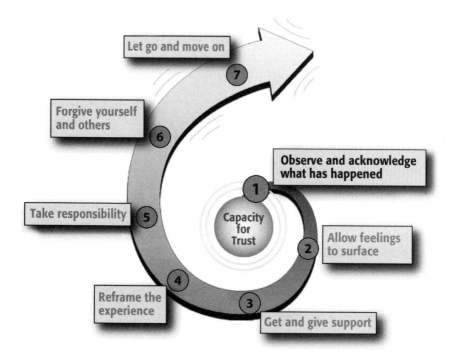

"*The distance is nothing; it is only **the first step** that is difficult.*"

—Marie de Vichy-Chamrond,
the Marquise du Deffand,
French woman of letters

"I couldn't get over what had happened. It was as if someone punched me in the gut. I was shocked that my boss took credit for work I had done so that she would look good in the eyes of the executive team."

Betrayal hurts, and so does being let down, disappointed, or frustrated when the people you work with break the trust you have in them. The larger the breach, the greater the hurt. Observing and acknowledging how trust has been broken represents the first Step in the healing process. In this Step, you become conscious and aware of your thoughts and feelings about what happened. The opposite of awareness is denial. You cannot heal that which you are ignoring, denying, or rationalizing away. In this way, the first Step of rebuilding trust raises your self-awareness. Your partner in this Step is courage: the courage to be honest with yourself and see situations for what they are.

> *The opposite of awareness is denial.*

No matter if you have been hurt or if you have hurt another, you start healing broken trust by observing how trust has been broken and acknowledging the impact of the breach.

Observing what has happened involves noticing the obvious and the not-so-obvious actions and behaviors that have transpired. A major betrayal such as a badly handled large-scale layoff is pretty obvious and may be what everybody is talking about. But just as harmful are the little things that add up and become big—things like snippets of gossip, which can add up to damage someone's reputation, and missed deadlines, which ultimately let others down. Remember to look for those patterns, too.

Acknowledging the impact includes recognizing what you and others are experiencing. Often people experience the impact of betrayal as a loss: the loss of what was or the loss of what could have been. You may be experiencing something as severe as the loss of a relationship, the loss of opportunity, or the loss of performance and results. Or, you may recognize that the breach of trust has resulted in the loss of *complete* confidence in someone else, so that you become more cautious in how you work with that person. You may also sense the loss of energy, confidence, and commitment that are telltale signs of broken trust.

The impact of a trust-breaking situation and the feelings associated with the loss vary in intensity depending on a number of factors. The person who breaks trust often underestimates the negative power of her behavior on the receiver. She may think, "Yes, I made a mistake, but what is the big deal?" A minor situation may feel like a big deal to someone if it surfaces unresolved feelings from a past betrayal. Impact is also proportional to the significance of the relationship involved. A minor letdown by an individual you work with for a few days will not hit you as hard as a significant betrayal you experience with someone you have collaborated with for years.

When You Have Been Betrayed

Kerri had been the Vice President for External Development for a prominent medical research center for eight years. During her tenure, she had developed deep relationships with people throughout the organization. Her team members, including Event Coordinator Kim, had a great deal of respect for her and cared about her deeply as a person. In short, they trusted her.

The entire team grew terribly concerned when Kerri became so ill that she needed to take a medical leave of absence. During her leave, they rose to the occasion to ensure that the team's performance did not skip a beat. For two months, Kim and the others did whatever was necessary to manage key deliverables and to sustain the team's spirit. They willingly chose to do whatever was necessary, out of team spirit and caring for their boss. They did not want Kerri to worry about work. They missed her and looked forward to her returning healthy.

Eventually, Kerri did return to work and the team welcomed her back.

A few weeks later while at a conference, Kim chatted with a colleague from another medical research center. During the course of the conversation, Kim learned that Kerri had been consulting to that organization while on medical leave. Kim just could not imagine that this story was true.

Dismayed, Kim called Kerri. She could not believe her ears when Kerri confirmed that the story was true. In that moment, Kim felt as though the rug had been pulled out from under her. The last two months flashed by before her eyes. She thought of the family dinners she had been late for, the Saturday morning soccer games she missed, the early morning arrivals to get a head start on the day and, above all, the prayers she had said in support of her boss's recovery. Kim felt taken advantage of, used, and manipulated. It was clear to her that she did not have the kind of relationship with Kerri she thought she did.

Kerri and Kim had worked together for eight years. For Kim, her relationship with Kerri was one of significance. Kerri was her trusted leader, advisor, and mentor. Because of that closeness, this betrayal impacted her quite deeply.

Your first step in healing is to acknowledge and observe what happened and the impact on you and the relationship. Pay attention to your inner experience, your questions and feelings, and add them up. Doing so will help you to *consciously observe* the situation, almost as if from the outside. You will *witness* what happened. Then you can put words on what you see: "Kerri broke the trust I thought we had in our relationship." Or even, "Kerri took advantage of me and the team." Either way, Kim ends up significantly disappointed. The next box walks you through how to observe this common outcome of broken trust.

Sometimes when you are in pain, you may have difficulty understanding where your feelings are coming from. You may ask, "What happened? What was that about?" When you hurt, you may also find yourself pulling back, withdrawing, and shutting down.

In such moments, you can begin to *acknowledge the impact* of the situation. For instance, the impact on Kim was so great that she began questioning her own perceptions and judgment. Betrayal

Observe Your Disappointment

Disappointment related to broken trust can lead to feelings of disenchantment that dissolve your commitment to your organization's mission and your connection to co-workers. Some disappointment may be a result of current organizational dynamics; some of the disappointment may be deeper-seated, stemming from old patterns learned during childhood. Either way, it is important to ask yourself, "What exactly am I feeling disappointed about?" "What is contributing to my letdown?"

Use these reflection questions to help you listen to where your pain is coming from:

? Is it a lack of appreciation for all your efforts?

Is it a lack of confidence in your competence?

Is it a lack of understanding or misunderstanding of what you are trying to accomplish?

Is it a lack of acknowledgment of who you are and what you have to offer?

One of the most subtle and yet insidious betrayals you can experience is not being fully seen or heard for who you really are. Not being recognized for your contribution to others and to the company hurts at an innate level. It takes courage to face and work through such pain.

touches you at your core when it causes you to question you own perceptions and judgment.

Have you ever been in a similar situation and asked yourself these questions:

? How could I have been so foolish?

How could I have not seen this?

How could I have trusted someone who would behave in such as manner?

This process involves acknowledging the strain or loss and feelings you are experiencing. Let's take a look at how some people we've worked with have observed common trust-breaking workplace behaviors and tease out the impact in terms of feelings and experience of loss:

- "My boss keeps giving me tasks at the end of the day, knowing that I don't have to leave at a certain time to pick up children. She always leaves at 5 P.M. on the dot and I end up staying until 8 P.M. Those extra hours cut into my personal life. I feel taken advantage of."

  — *"I am agitated."*

  — *"I feel put-upon."*

  — *"I wonder if this is the place for me."*

  → Loss of commitment

- He told me that working on this project would increase my visibility with management. But then he presented it without acknowledging or crediting my work. He double-crossed me. I lost the opportunity to demonstrate my competence."

  — *"I was cut off."*

  — *"I feel used."*

  — *"I wonder what I did to deserve this."*

  → Loss of confidence

- "I arrive at meetings on time, but my co-worker is consistently ten to fifteen minutes late. It seems as though she thinks that what she has to do is more important than what I have to do. I don't think she is respecting my time or the importance of the job I have to do."

  — *"I feel disrespected."*

  — *"I'm frustrated and disappointed."*

  — *"I feel insulted and devalued."*

  → Loss of commitment to the relationship

- "My colleague assured me repeatedly that he would deliver his part of the project on time. When we were down to the wire, he didn't come through. Three of us had to scramble late into the night to meet our deadline."

— *"I feel let down."*

— *"I am embarrassed."*

— *"I feel taken advantage of."*

Loss of complete confidence in a colleague

- "I've worked for this company since its inception, sacrificing my weekends, pay, and benefits during the startup phase. Now we're up and running and they've 'eliminated' my job and me along with it. I gave my best to this company, and this is what I get?"

— *"I am extremely disappointed."*

— *"I feel used."*

— *"I am scared about the future."*

Loss of confidence in self

Left unacknowledged, the impact of any of these experiences can fester and deteriorate into more serious sentiments, such as:

— *"I feel betrayed."*

— *"I'm depressed."*

— *"I'm worthless."*

— *"I feel vulnerable."*

— *"I feel like hell!"*

— *"I just don't care anymore."*

— *"I give up!"*

— *"I will get back at them."*

Loss of energy

Do any of these examples of behaviors that break trust sound familiar? Are you able to acknowledge your letdown?

At this stage, don't try to analyze, understand, or intellectualize your thoughts and feelings—simply "notice" them. You don't need to come up with solutions or resolutions right now. This Step is about giving yourself permission to be honest with yourself as you observe and acknowledge what is so.

When You Have Betrayed Others

We all have experienced being betrayed by others. And, the truth is, we all have betrayed others as well. It takes inner strength to look at ourselves in the mirror and courageously

> *We all have betrayed others. We don't mean to hurt others, but we do.*

see how we have hurt or let others down—often without even knowing it. We don't mean to hurt others, but we do. At work, we hurt our co-workers. At home, we hurt our spouses and other loved ones. We are most often unaware or unconscious of the mistakes we make, but they still damage the trust within our relationships. Michelle lived through such an experience several years ago:

> *I had developed a very close relationship with my coach, Georgia. Over time, the relationship grew into a friendship. During an extended week-end trip, Dennis and I were visiting Georgia and her husband, Drew, at their home. Drew performed in a band on weekends and had made arrangements for us to attend his gig.*
>
> *The first day we were there, Dennis and I visited his alma mater, which was outside the city where Georgia and Drew lived. While there, we were invited to a special alumni business-network-ing meeting. "Great opportunity for making business contacts! There will be people there who want to meet you," we were told by the alumni office representative. But the event was on the same night we were to see Drew perform. We were so excited about the special evening with Georgia and Drew. And, we were presented with a business opportunity to make the kinds of contacts so impor-*

tant for our early-stage business. We began to troubleshoot. Maybe there was a way we could go to both events? Perhaps we could join Georgia at Drew's performance a bit later in the evening?

I shared the presenting opportunity and posed these questions to Georgia. It seemed simple and straightforward to me. I thought Georgia, as my coach, would surely have considered the idea positively or seen some creative solutions. Yet her immediate reaction was just the opposite: distant coldness, glaring stares, and painful silence. When I observed that I had inadvertently offended her, I retracted the question and apologized profusely.

I felt sick to my stomach. I had to face the truth that while my actions were unintentional, with that one question, I had unintentionally broken her trust and she felt betrayed. She was deeply hurt by me and consequently shut down. I had lost a person and a relationship that were special to me.

When you have hurt another person, observing and acknowledging involves honestly facing the truth about how you have betrayed others—even, and especially, if you did so inadvertently, unintentionally, maybe even unconsciously. A perceived intention may breach trust, even if action does not occur. Michelle only contemplated the

---

 Reflection Question
When might you have unintentionally betrayed others?

---

possibility of arriving late for Drew's performance. While that consideration was not carried out, the intent implied in the consideration contributed to a breach of trust. For Georgia, Michelle's consideration implied that attending Drew's performance and spending the evening together was not as special to Michelle as it was for Georgia. Further, Georgia concluded that the relationship in general was not as significant to Michelle as it was to her. When people hurt, sometimes they are inclined to draw such exaggerated, illogical conclusions stemming from their pain.

Pay Attention to Signs of Betrayal

Have you ever withdrawn and shut down as a result of disappointment? Your own experience and reaction to being hurt helps you to understand that of others. Often the people you betray are not able to talk to you about what is going on. You may need, therefore, to look for subtle and not so subtle signs that tell you someone is hurt:

> **?** Is he visibly upset? Is her head down? Is he avoiding eye contact? Are there tears in her eyes?
>
> Is he abrupt or short or exhibiting other signs of anger?
>
> Is she unusually quiet, pulled back and reserved toward you?
>
> Is he unresponsive? Ignoring or shunning you?

Once you are able to observe these signs, you can then pay attention to them. You pay attention by sharing your observations and asking questions to help you understand what is behind these reactions and how you may have contributed to the situation.

Healing is a process of inquiry. Your questions guide the process. Share what you see and ask questions for understanding.

> *"I have the impression that you are upset. Have I done something to hurt you? If I have, I would like to know."*
>
> *"I am aware that I may have let you down. I want to understand how my behavior impacted you."*
>
> *"You appear to be pulling back. I would like to understand what is contributing to it and what part I had in it."*
>
> *"I see that you are hurt. I am aware that I was abrupt yesterday and may have offended you. Is that true?"*
>
> *"I have noticed a shift in our working relationship. I am having a hard time reaching you and have the impression that you are avoiding me. Have I done something to let you down?"*
>
> *"I sense a shift in our interactions. I experience you being abrupt, which is highly unusual. What is going on? Did I do something to disturb you?"*

When you share your observations and ask questions with a genuine willingness to understand your part in a situation, the door to healing opens.

Respond to What Others Say

Chances are, you'll feel unsettled when you hear how you inadvertently or accidently let someone down. The situation may be so significant that you feel knocked off your feet. If that's the case, simply listen for now, and let the person know that you want to understand the situation before you respond. If you react when you are ungrounded, you're likely to surface feelings or abdicate responsibility and inadvertently breach trust again. Instead, take some time for yourself. Allow your feelings to surface, get support, reframe the situation, and determine your responsibility (Steps Two through Five). Then, you'll be prepared to acknowledge your responsibility, ask forgiveness, and move forward in the relationship.

In less significant situations and with practice, you may be able to move through the Steps very quickly. If so, you may choose to react immediately to what the person you let down says by *sharing* how this awareness has impacted you.

> *"I really blew it. I hate that my failure to deliver as promised created significant hardship on you. I feel embarrassed and am sorry for how my failure to keep our agreement impacted you."*

> *"I understand how I behaved in a self-serving way during that meeting. How could I have been so self-centered as to have completely ignored your needs? I feel ashamed of myself."*

> *"I now regret pushing so hard to finish that project; the cost to you, me, and others was too great. I am so sorry."*

Through self-exploration and acknowledgement, negative feelings begin to subside. You are on a path of renewal that will restore the essential trust in your relationships.

Observing Signs of Broken Trust and Its Impact

Here are some examples of how people we have worked with have *observed* workplace betrayals and expressed their feelings regarding the *impact* of those breaches:

Observation: "As a 30+ year veteran of this company, I could teach these young supervisors a lot, but they think they know it all, just because they have a college education. They talk to me like I don't know anything."

Impact: "I feel underutilized and devalued. When I go, everything I know goes with me."

Observation: "Management calls people at the last minute to change schedules or ask us to work overtime or double shifts. These requests come out of the blue. I am not able to make plans to be with my family, to have a personal life."

Impact: "I feel devalued; that I do not count. I feel management does not care about me. I wonder why I should care about them or the organization?"

Observation: "I am noticing sloppy work and mistakes happening more frequently. I don't see signs of things improving."

Impact: "I really don't care anymore. I come in, I do the basic work that is required of me, and I go home. I see a growing sense of hopelessness and helplessness."

Observation: "When an operator makes a mistake and an accident happens, management lists them as 'behavior problems' and they are told to go to 'counseling.' This reaction implies blame and assumes the employee is 100 percent at fault. As a result, people attempt to cover up mistakes or injuries."

Impact: "People feel vulnerable with the process and wonder why they aren't invited to discuss and problem-solve so the same mistake/accident won't happen again."

Observation: "My supervisor is constantly looking over my shoulder in a search for mistakes. I feel she does not trust me to do my job."

Impact: "As a result, there is a growing sense of tension, stress, and fear between us."

When You Want to Help Others Rebuild Trust

*"A life is not **important** except in the **impact** it has on other lives."*
—Jackie Robinson
Hall of Fame baseball player

Have you observed other people's behavior that has caused trust to erode? As someone on the outside of the behavior pattern, you can play a very powerful role in observing what has happened and helping people to acknowledge the impact. Chances are that you can see that which the betrayed and betrayer cannot, because they are blinded by pain or guilt.

To fully *observe* what is happening, start by raising your periscope. Look for the subtle signs of distrust, such as low energy or enthusiasm, lack of confidence, and/or unwillingness to commit. The box on page 28 captures verbatim comments of people we have worked with as they express these signs and acknowledge their impact.

Pay attention to what specific actions, activities, and events may be building and breaking trust. Be careful not to overlook small, subtle signs of distrust, such as people coming late to meetings, missing appointments, avoiding speaking directly to individuals, gossiping, and backbiting.

>> **Trust Tip**   *The healing process starts with awareness. Observing and acknowledging people's concerns regarding an action and the impact of that action are the first Steps of the process.*

Find out what is important to people. Listen to what they are saying in the hallways, the break rooms, and on the shop floor. Consider what is most important to pay attention to. Listen with compassion, without judging, rationalizing, or blaming. People in pain need to be heard and understood.

You may be the first to acknowledge that trust has been broken. People don't care how much you know until they know how much you care. Articulating the truth shows them that you genuinely care and creates a safe container for healing. You will name "the elephant in the room:" behavior that is obvious but that no one is talking about. Because you are one

> *People don't care how much you know until they know how much you care.*

step removed from the situation, you can offer words to describe the behavior; one of those words might be betrayal. The very act of acknowledging the breach of trust helps bring it to the surface where healing can start.

As we have indicated, it is important to acknowledge the impact of the betraying behavior. Ask the person who experienced betrayal to identify what she experienced. Help her articulate the impact and recognize the feelings of loss she is experiencing. The box gives you an easy-to-use framework to help people express the impact they are feeling.

At times, the way you acknowledge betrayal may be to step in when you see a pattern repeating. You can speak up when certain colleagues are always late to meetings, never get projects in on time,

---

Reflection Question

What do you see and hear regarding what people are concerned about in your workplace?

---

or hold up the team's progress because their piece is often incomplete. It takes courage to acknowledge a behavior that is hurting rather than supporting others. To stop the cycle of betrayal begetting betrayal, have essential conversations in private, share your observations, and seek to understand where others are coming from. In so doing, you are helping others to become more self-aware. What is important is to intervene with caring and compassion versus judgment and blame. Judging others only creates greater pain. No one wants to be judged.

A Framework for Helping Others Observe and Acknowledge Betrayal

You can play an effective role in helping others to rebuild trust by assisting them in observing and acknowledging that which they may be unable to see due to their pain, guilt, or denial.

Our friend and colleague, Rob Goldberg, offers a simple framework that we adapted. Use it with those you are trying to help observe a trust-breaking situation and acknowledge its impact:

1. **When:** Encourage the parties to describe the *situation or context* regarding when and where the trust-breaking situation took place. Ask them to be specific. An answer may sound like:

   Last Wednesday when we were in our morning team meeting discussing the necessary resources each member needed to complete their part of the team project, . . .

2. **What:** Ask them to describe the behavior concerning the actions they observed, listing specific behavior, not inferences:

   You spoke for 25 minutes of the allotted 30-minute time slot for our topic. Most of your material was about your personal needs and negated the interests of others.

   OR

   I spoke for 25 minutes of the allotted 30-minute time slot for our topic. I covered my needs in depth.

3. **How:** Instruct them to express the impact of the behavior on them. Help them to understand what was lost by the behavior.

   I felt irritated that I did not have an opportunity to voice my needs or express my concerns regarding my part of the project. I noticed a number of the other team members pull away from the table and disengage from the discussion for the rest of the meeting.

   OR

   When I noticed a number of team members pull away from the table and disengage from the discussion for the rest of the meeting, I sensed that I had created that distance. I felt badly for having taken up so much of the time. I realized that I had essentially "stolen" the meeting for my own purposes. In so doing, I had silenced others' thoughts and taken away their opportunity to advocate for their needs. I lost my trusted position within the team.

When you courageously raise awareness of behavior that is not healthy, you actually honor yourself and the relationships around you. You help to cultivate an environment of trust and renewal.

2

Allow Feelings to Surface

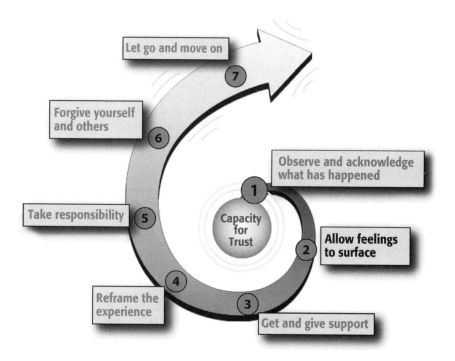

"Feelings are not supposed to be logical. Dangerous is the man who has rationalized his emotions."

—David Borenstein
Polish artist

In the first of the Seven Steps, you opened your eyes and ears to observe a situation of broken trust and acknowledge its impact. Step Two is about opening your heart. Everyone—including the person who unintentionally or even intentionally hurts another—has feelings about a disappointment, letdown, or betrayal. Those feelings can range from a quiet sense of vulnerability and hesitation to a deep pain. And everyone is entitled to have and honor those feelings.

The second of the Seven Steps—allowing those feelings to rise to the surface—often comes as a "package" with Step One, where courage was your partner. Now, with compassion as your partner, you become fully aware of—and present to—your feelings so that healing can begin.

People we work with often experience Step Two as the "messiest" Step. Feelings surface in visceral and sometimes physical ways. Because surfacing feelings exposes your vulnerability, you may feel sad and discouraged in this Step. The Seven Steps for Healing graphic captures this sensation by depicting this Step plunging down—just like your energy. But like the graphic, you'll start to emerge from this difficult place in Step Three. The support you'll find there will be your stepping-stone to move into reframing the experience and find the lessons inherent in your situation.

While all of the Seven Steps are important, Step Two is perhaps the most important for true healing and renewal. Feelings do not go away by themselves and time alone will not heal pain. You cannot heal that which you have not expressed, most importantly to yourself. When you do not allow yourself to express your feelings, you fail to acknowledge yourself and the impact of a situation. In that way, you betray *yourself*. Un-surfaced and unresolved feelings may then hold you back professionally and personally, even years later. How?

- You may overreact to situations, leaving your co-workers scratching their heads and your boss wondering if she can trust you in high-pressure situations.

- You may be inclined to shift blame to others or your organization for a responsibility that is yours to own. It's likely that much of the lost employee satisfaction, eroding levels of engagement, and declining cultural health that many organizations face are the result of unresolved hurts, disappointments, or emotions that were left to ferment after a betrayal situation.

- You may be more likely perpetuate the cycle of betrayal and end up hurting people who were not involved in the original situation. Issues from home might seep into your work relationships, and problems at work may surface at home.

- You may hurt yourself by engaging in behavior that hurts others. Case in point: gossip, which is one particular form of reactionary betrayal. Un-surfaced feelings tend to seep out when you talk about situations behind people's backs. If you participate in such behavior, you impact the reputation of others and you ruin your reputation as being trustworthy.

- You run the risk of becoming a prisoner to the victim posture and the anger, bitterness, resentment and, ultimately, apathy, that come with that posture. These emotions will cloud your thinking, burden your heart, sink your spirits, and de-energize your body. When you remain a victim, you lose your confidence to act, your commitment to go the distance, and your personal power to do what you have the potential to accomplish.

In short, if you do not allow your feelings to surface, the hurt will live on inside you, taking up "space" that you could otherwise use for connection and compassion towards others. When you are in pain, you contract and begin to lose touch with yourself. You may forget who you really are and what you have to offer others. In that way, you cut yourself off from healing, relationships, and yourself. Ultimately, you betray yourself.

But if you do allow your feelings to surface, you will begin to heal. It's likely that you will notice a release as your feelings come out. Many times, people describe that release in physical terms (as described in the box on page 35).

Some other aspects of the release are:

- The pain inside you will begin to subside.

- You will feel yourself open up, and your doubts will begin to ease.

- You may have the peaceful sensation of returning to yourself; feelings are the window to your soul, and you will have opened up that window. You will remember who you are and what you have to bring to the situation.

> *Feelings are the window to your soul.*

- You see "light at the end of the tunnel" and believe that hope can take the place of hurt. Only when you have hope can you reconnect with yourself, reconnect with others in empathy, and thus fulfill your highest purpose at work and in your life.

- You become aware of that which is asking to be healed. Your released feelings let you know what you need in terms of support (Step Three) and guide you to a place in which you can reframe the situation and take responsibility.

The release makes room for you to learn from the experience. Insights and life lessons will come as you embrace the possibilities inherent in healing.

Because feelings come in waves, you're likely to return to this Step as you progress through subsequent Steps. Remember, healing is not a linear process. You will experience emotions in each of the Seven Steps. We often use the metaphor of the onion: when you peel back the layers of an onion, you cry. It's the same with healing. As you move through the process and peel back the layers of the hurt and disappointment that come with broken trust, you may get in touch with subsequent waves of emotion. As you do, you are releasing your pain and making room for renewal.

Ways to Surface Your Feelings

The process of allowing your feelings to surface is essentially the same whether someone else hurt you or if you were the one to hurt another. Coming to terms with your feelings is personal work that

Physical Pain, Physical Release

People we talk with often describe physical symptoms associated with feeling betrayed, such as:

"I have knots in my stomach."

"My heart is literally aching."

"My head is pounding."

"I feel dizzy and light-headed."

"My shoulders are so tight they hurt."

"I always feel like I'm going to throw up."

"My legs have started twitching."

Many figurative descriptions that we've heard also have to do with a body in pain:

"I feel like someone punched me in the stomach."

"He knocked me off my feet."

"It was as if she kicked me in the teeth."

"It's gut-wrenching pain."

"I feel like someone has ripped my insides out."

Likewise, a release often comes in a physical form. When you allow your feelings to rise to the surface, you may feel:

- A releasing of tension in your neck and shoulders
- Knots untying in your upset stomach
- The ability to breathe more deeply
- Lighter in your heart
- Clearer in your head
- More stable on your feet
- Grounded in your body

Reflection Question

What feelings are surfacing for you as you read this section?

nobody else can do for you; there is no one-size-fits-all model for how to get in touch with your feelings. What this Step "looks like" will vary depending on the severity of the breach of trust and your personal preferences.

Essentially, you need to give yourself room and permission to feel your feelings. When you allow your feelings to surface, you honor your relationship with yourself. If you feel anger, give voice

> If you feel anger, give voice to your anger. If you feel afraid, pay attention to your fear and vulnerability.

to your anger. If you feel afraid, pay attention to your fear and vulnerability. If you are grieving the loss of a relationship, it is okay to be sad— even very, very sad. The more significant the relationship, the deeper the sadness. Know that it is okay to be in pain.

Self-Reflection

In our experience, Step Two always involves some kind of a pause. When people are in pain, they tend to keep busy, as if to say, "If I keep moving, I can avoid facing my hurt." That approach doesn't work. You need to pause and reconnect with yourself. This pause may be moments, hours, days, or weeks. Sometimes you may need to take time off, as one of our clients, Marisol, did when she was faced with a hurtful situation that knocked her off her feet:

> *Marisol, a well-respected manager who had been identified as a strong performer with high potential, was given the opportunity to serve on a year-long special project team. She gave her all to this out-of-town, full-time assignment, and when the time came to plan her next move within the company, she spoke to her division head about a promotion.*
>
> *The division head explained that she wasn't in line for a promotion because he had received feedback that her performance on the special project had been "substandard." Members of the team had complained about her.*

Ways We Access and Release Our Feelings

Michelle has learned that she needs to complete a three-part process to get in touch with her feelings when she has been let down. Physical motion that has a reflective component helps her wrestle with what is eating at her. Then, quiet time to meditate provides insight. Michelle's path is a rigorous swim or brisk walk in nature to shake loose her inner tension, and then sitting quietly in meditation followed by a hot cup of tea and writing in her journal to capture her feelings.

Dennis utilizes a combination of physical movement and different types of reflection exercises to access and release his feelings. For physical movement, he does an eclectic form of stretching, and some kind of cardiovascular workout such as running, swimming, hiking and biking, or cross-country skiing in winter. For reflection, he practices yoga, meditation, prayer, and journal writing daily, and periodically discusses key issues with a coach.

This news came as a complete shock to Marisol. She simply couldn't get over the fact that none of her team members had spoken to her directly and that her boss had not brought their dissatisfaction to her personal attention. "What else are people not telling me?" she wondered.

Reeling, Marisol took two weeks off. In addition to reaching out to her medical doctor, therapist, and career advisor for support, she spent time alone walking, thinking, and writing. She allowed herself to feel the anger, hurt, and deep vulnerability emerge to a level that would have been difficult for her if she had continued with life as usual.

A pause gives you time for self-reflection. You find quiet time when you can allow yourself to feel your feelings and express them to yourself. You *connect* with yourself. Many people find that activities such as meditation, journal writing, or some form of physical movement help them reflect; we've described our personal processes in the box above. What's important is that you ask yourself the following questions out loud, in the privacy of your own space with uninter-rupted time:

? What am I feeling right now?

What sensations am I feeling in my body right now?

Where am I feeling tension or tightness?

What feelings related to my tension would I like to express right now?

Physical Expression

Because healing feelings is a visceral experience, the process to bring them forward may be quite physical. Sometimes, the expression of feelings may be instinctive and immediate. While fishing one Sat-urday afternoon, one manager we worked with learned of a hurtful work situation via an e-mail on his Blackberry. He swore out loud and then threw his phone into the river!

Depending on the intensity of your pain, shouting, screaming, or crying may all be ways you let your feelings out. It goes without saying that there is a time and place for these kinds of reactions, and you'll want to find an appropriate, and perhaps private, place to sur-face your feelings. Sometimes, constructive physical ways of express-ing feelings—such as running hard, whacking a bucket of balls at the driving range, kickboxing, weightlifting, or volunteering to smash glass at a recycling center—can bring about a release.

Talk It Out

Sometimes, people need to talk with someone in order to surface feel-ings. You may have a trusted coach, counselor, colleague, friend, or family member who can be there for you. If so, that's great. If not, and you would like to find one, reach out for support as described in Step Three, which often goes hand-in-hand with this part of Step Two.

Your organization may provide venues to talk about your feel-ings. Professionally facilitated focus groups, time with coaches, and

Crying

Society sends the message that adults, especially men, shouldn't show their feelings. We learn at an early age that "big boys don't cry" and tears at work are out of line.

We've led hundreds of workshops to rebuild trust in organizations. Time and time again, someone cries when we get to the part about allowing feelings to surface. When a person does, a sense of compassion comes into the room. That person is saying, "I feel safe with you, I am entrusting my feelings to you, I am letting you see how hurt I am." That person who cries honors himself and extends a significant privilege to those around him.

Dennis recently was speaking in a large hotel ballroom. He was telling a story related to these Seven Steps for Healing when a woman shared her painful experiences. A sacred stillness enshrouded members of the audience as they attentively listened to her. In her tears, people were able to connect to their own pain. Many welled up with emotion themselves.

When you are fully present with your feelings and you open up your heart, you may cry, too—and that is okay. Your tears allow you to access your soul.

even anonymous surveys represent opportunities for you to express how you feel about trust-breaking situations in the workplace.

When You Have Been Betrayed

I was livid! Yet, deep down I was really hurting. I hated Mitch, my co-worker, for what he had done to me, and I despised myself for being so naïve that I didn't see it coming. All day long my head was throbbing and I couldn't concentrate on my work. At lunch, I couldn't eat; my stomach was in knots.

I knew I needed to do something to surface my pain. So after work I headed to the gym, got on my kickboxing gear, and pounded the punching bag until I dropped from exhaustion. Afterwards, I felt bushed, but better, and was able to think through my options more clearly.

Writing to Surface Your Feelings

Writing can be a way to get in touch with and express your feelings. It is a way to put what happened into words and release buried feelings visually.

Stream-of-consciousness or free writing is writing for a fixed time period (perhaps 20 to 30 minutes) without stopping.

Tips for Free Writing

- Forget everything you learned about how to write.

- Put your pen or pencil to paper and begin writing. Don't think about what you are writing. Feel free to cut loose and write whatever comes up regarding what happened.

- This writing is for you: don't worry about getting it right or editing your work. Don't reread and censor what you wrote; your words do not need to make sense to anyone else. The purpose is to release your feelings.

- If you run out of things to say, repeat the last statement you wrote. Repeat it until something new surfaces, taking you to a deeper level of writing and release.

- If you are still out of words, try drawing until the timer goes off. When the allotted time is over, stop.

This process of writing can bring up strong emotions, so it is important to release feelings in layers, one at a time. We have found using a timer with a specific timeframe to write helps create a safe container in which there is a beginning and an end.

Adapted from Laura Davis, *The Courage to Heal Workbook*[1]

When you are hurt, you need to find a way to let your feelings out. If physical exercise isn't your outlet, try one or more of the other methods covered here. Through those methods or through the writing exercise explained in the box above, you become able to surface your underlying feelings related to disappointment, letdown, or betrayal.

While sometimes you can process your emotions with the person or persons who hurt you, many times this is not possible, for a host

---

Dealing with Guilt

People tend to relive betrayals in their minds a thousand times. If you are like many people who are hard on yourself, you may become obsessed with guilt and worry: *"I shouldn't have _____"* or *"I wish I hadn't _____."* Such thoughts are of no positive value and do not support healing. They drain your energy, cloud your thinking, and clutter your emotions. When you replay the situation over and over, you hurt *yourself* in addition to the person you betrayed. So say *"no"* to negative guilt. Use that time inside yourself to take positive responsibility to feel your feelings instead.

---

of reasons. The person may, by choice, not be available for discussion. She may just want to move on. He may be shut down and checked out. She may not be willing to take ownership or responsibility for her part in the betrayal, an avoidance mechanism that in and of itself is a further breach of trust. Or, he may not be able or willing to work it through with you because he is not as aware or in the same healing stage as you are.

When You Have Betrayed Others

Nina was one of the very few people who managed to move between divisions of a large corporation located in the city in which she lived. She made a name for herself and "climbed the ladder" while making the kind of valuable connections that opened doors such as this latest assignment.

In her new job, Nina looked for opportunities to connect with her new colleagues to find her place. Because she was very observant and easy to talk to, she began to develop relationships quickly. Soon, people were confiding in her.

One of those people was Ted. He, like Nina, was excited to advance his career. He told Nina that he had applied for a job in a sister company.

The next day, Nina was in a meeting with her boss, Evan, to whom Ted reported as well. Evan presented a short list of people he wanted to put forward for the job in the other division. "Ted has applied for that job, too," Nina blurted to demonstrate that she was "in the know."

Evan hadn't known of Ted's intentions. In that moment, Nina had betrayed Ted's confidence. When he found out, Ted was angry and hurt, and distanced Nina completely.

Nina was filled with remorse. She cried over her mistake, and asked herself repeatedly, "How could I have done that to Ted?" She withdrew from the connections she had made, lost sight of her strengths and confidence, felt shame, and came face-to-face with her vulnerability.

When Nina recounted this story to Michelle, tears came to her eyes—even though it happened over twenty years ago.

When you betray another person, the first person you betray is yourself. The betrayal of "the self" can be the most painful form of betrayal. It never feels good to see that you compromised your own integrity, as Nina did when she violated Ted's confidence. When you begin to acknowledge to yourself that you have indeed betrayed a person close to you, you definitely have feelings.

Those feelings, which are often named guilt, remorse, shame, and embarrassment, need to be surfaced and dealt with. Until you allow your feelings to surface, and work through them, you will not be emotionally available to hear the person you hurt, take responsibility, learn, and move on. As you allow the feelings associated with your role to rise to the surface, you may find that other, more deep-seated feelings come up as well. For Nina, it was her vulnerability that surfaced.

This is the time for you to get in touch with your feelings. You are coming face-to-face with your own humanness: You made a mistake and your actions hurt another. Be open to the emotions that surface and be vulnerable. When you are vulnerable, you are in a precious space to feel your pain, and hear and feel the other person's pain. You are most open for healing to take place. As you move through those feelings, you will regain your footing and a sense of being grounded will return.

It is your responsibility to work through your pain. It clearly is not the burden of those you betrayed. Filled with remorse, betrayers often run back to the betrayed and try to work through the feelings with the person they hurt. Resist the temptation to approach him or her until you are fully ready to take responsibility, as described in Step Five.

When You Want to Help Others Rebuild Trust

Have you ever had an experience when someone reacted with intensity much greater than the incident at hand? You and those around you were so thrown by the intensity of the person's emotions that you wondered, "What in the heck just happened?"

Un-surfaced, misplaced feelings that your co-workers bring into the workplace can derail your workgroup's performance and well-being. Perhaps you want to help because of the effect those un-surfaced feelings are having on your team's productivity. Or maybe your intention is to help the individual who is acting out her hurt.

Either way, as someone who wants to help, your role isn't to have all of the answers. In this Step, which is about *allowing feelings to surface*, your role is to create a safe environment, be present, and listen. You are not expected to resolve the feelings for others. No one can resolve another's feelings. When you simply hold a compassionate space, the channels for healing will open and feelings will surface. Because the approaches you will take will vary depending on the number of people you are trying to help, we've split the advice into two sections: when you want to help one person, and when you want to help an entire team.

Helping One Person

We have learned that at times people who are feeling betrayed or coming to terms with having betrayed another just need some one-on-one time with someone who cares. Thirty minutes over a cup of

Helping Another Surface Feelings

The role of the helper is to support another individual to express his or her feelings in order to work through the pain. These best practices will help you to support someone to surface feelings:

Clarify your intentions

Be clear that you are there to support him, not to advocate your own agenda.

Create a safe space

Find an appropriate place and uninterrupted time so she can be free to allow her feelings to surface and feel comfortable enough to do so.

Be present

Give your undivided attention to allow him to express himself fully. Sometimes all someone needs is to be heard and seen for who he is.

Listen

Totally listen to what she has to say without agreeing, taking sides, or making judgmental comments.

Ask questions

If he is stuck or reaches a plateau and you sense that there are more feelings that need to surface, come from a place of inquiry. Ask questions that will elicit responses:

? What else are you feeling?

Are there other feelings that need to come out?

What will help you to surface those emotions?

---

coffee can nurture significant movement. At this stage in the process, when emotions are very raw and just coming to the surface, it's very important to find a private space to have these conversations.

Your role in this Step is to provide an opportunity for the person you are helping to express the impact of the trust-breaking situation: to talk it through, vent frustrations, and express disappointment or anger. Resist the temptation to say, "Everything will be fine" or some other expression to get the person to positive emotions.

Some phrases that do work at this stage are:

"It's okay to let it all out."

"It is okay to vent your frustrations."

"Tell me about it."

"You don't have to make sense: just say whatever comes up."

"I'm here for you."

"Whatever you say or do will be between us; I know you are hurting."

Helping a Group

Perhaps you are in a position to help a group of people, be they co-workers, teammates, subordinates, or internal "clients." A team or unit that shares a breach of trust may need to heal together. Giving group members constructive ways to discuss their feelings and experiences, whether on your own or through the use of an outside facilitator, helps them let go of the negativity they are holding.

In our work supporting organizations healing from broken trust, we use different kinds of tools and experiential exercises to help people identify, give voice to, and release their feelings. Several such tools are summarized in the box on the next page.

» *Trust Tip* *People have feelings regarding business decisions, particularly those that impact their jobs and their lives; the larger the changes, the greater the feelings. People's feelings don't go away by themselves: people need constructive forums in which to share their concerns.*

Sometimes, people have pain they are afraid or feel unable to share. When you compassionately give your attention to understanding others, you are letting them know that you respect their pain. You demonstrate that you care when you listen, observe, and acknowledge their experience of disappointment, letdown, or betrayal. This open availability is an important step to heal the wounds and rebuild trust.

Helping Groups Surface Feelings

These are some tools that can help a group to surface feelings around broken trust:

Mind Map

Lead a group discussion capturing key trust-related issues and people's feelings regarding those issues on a large diagram. Starting at the center, define key issues on different "branches." Have people express their feelings concerning each issue on "twigs" coming off each respective branch.

Betrayal Continuum

Capture people's perceptions regarding their frustrations, disappointments, and experiences of broken trust on a wall chart continuum from minor to major, unintentional to intentional (see the box on page 3 of the Introduction).

Rituals

Symbolic activities can help build and strengthen a sense of community within a team or organization and open up space for the sharing of feelings. For example, in a "Letting Go" exercise, ask group members to stand in a circle. Each writes down his or her feelings on paper and speaks them out loud, then releases them by tossing the paper into a trashcan in the center of the circle.

Surveys

The Reina Trust Building Institute has Individual, Leader, Team, and Organizational Trust Scales, which are valid and reliable instruments designed to measure interpersonal dynamics at various levels, surface people's concerns and feelings, and share their lived experiences regarding trust dynamics in a safe and anonymous way.

Get and Give Support

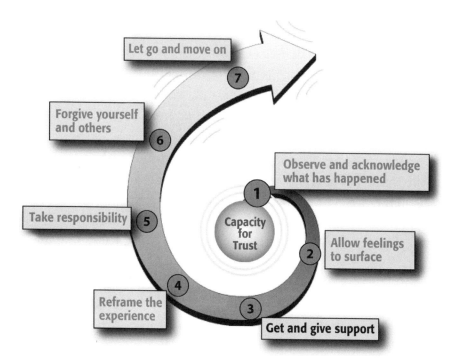

"*Be bold, and mighty forces will come to your aid.*"

—Johann Wolfgang von Goethe

Support is the vehicle through which you use the pain surfaced in the early Steps as a crucial stepping-stone to the learning, lightness, and letting go inherent in Steps Four through Seven. Support reminds you that betrayal can be a gift and provides tremendous opportunity for growth when you let yourself see it that way. Step Three of the Seven Steps for Healing is about how you can reach out to others for support, whether you are the betrayed or the inadvertent betrayer.

Many times, people surface their feelings and then stop the healing process. Support helps you to make a choice about the path to take. Courage is your partner when you embrace Step Three. You choose to move into and embrace your healing. Conversely, when you choose to linger in Steps One and Two, you embrace the stance of the victim. Healing to rebuild trust does not happen to you, it happens because of you, as a result of the conscious choice you make about how to respond to disappointment, hurt, or pain.

Over the last two decades, in supporting individuals, teams, and organizations to rebuild trust, we have accompanied some people who immediately embrace the path of healing, and others who linger in the victim mode, have false starts, or stop partway through. We honor their choices, no matter how circuitous their paths may be. What we caution them against is choosing to remain a victim. Why?

- They settle into resentment and bitterness. Over time, they take on an air of entitlement, feeling justified in what they feel the world "owes" them. These are not easy people to work with. When they don't get what they feel they are owed, they become apathetic and abdicate responsibility. They tend to go through the motions, doing only what is necessary to get by, and are masterful at covering their tracks.

  Does this description sound familiar to you? Are you this person? Do you work with someone like this? If yes, you are not alone. The workplace is filled with these "working wounded." Think of what it is like to collaborate with this individual.

- When people choose the path of healing, they step directly into their pain and choose to work through it instead of becoming defined by it. The result is renewal with heightened awareness of self, others, and what it takes to have healthy relationships that produce results.

- These individuals are conscious and aware of themselves and of others. They are as invested in others' success as they are in their own. They are inclined to take responsibility and hold themselves accountable. In short, they are trustworthy and you know that, with them, you can accomplish just about anything.

  Do these people sound familiar to you? Are some on your team? What is it like to collaborate with these people? Would you like to have more of them around you? Would you like to be a person who chooses this path?

Ways to Get Support

Support is a gift you give to yourself. Everyone, including the person who hurt someone else, is deserving of support. Many people, ashamed of their pain, let their pride stop them from reaching out. They deny themselves compassion. Asking for help is not a sign of weakness; support may, in fact, challenge you to go even deeper into your pain than you might on your own. In seeking support, you are extending compassion to yourself and honoring your humanness.

The role of support is to provide perspective that you may not see in your pain. Through support, you discover lessons. You come to understand your pain. Support comes in many forms, and the degree of support needed will vary depending on the circumstances: the more hurtful the betrayal, or the more unresolved the feelings that are left over from past betrayals, the greater the need for a strong framework of support.

Ask Others for Support

The most common way to garner support is to reach out to friends, family, colleagues, or professionals such as clergy members, coaches, consultants, facilitators, and Human Resources specialists. It's important to talk to someone with whom you feel safe. As one of our clients said, "The first place I went was to my wife and my minister . . . people who love me, warts and all." Support that fosters healing most effectively comes from a person who can remain neutral by suspending her own judgment and is someone you feel safe expressing your feelings to.

Your supporter's role is to:

- Help you to move through the Steps of acknowledging what happened, allowing your feelings to surface, and gaining objectivity to reframe your experience and take responsibility
- Hold the space of healing
- Hold you accountable compassionately

The sacred container of support is compromised if he or she:

- Tells you what to do
- Is judgmental toward you or the other person involved
- Engages in venting about what happened
- "Joins forces" with you by taking your side in a way that helps you stay stuck in blaming another: "That guy was a jerk to me just like he was to you! He was so wrong and you were right!"

You can also tap into communities of support such as "trust circles" and other safe forums with colleagues. Through hearing others' experiences, you come to understand your own. Expressing your

Reflection Question
How can you get the support you need?

feelings within a group to gain support for healing is not griping, whining, or moaning for the sake of blaming others or the organization. The focus of these groups is to seek support from others who are also willing to take responsibility for their behavior and for seeking solutions.

How to Ask for Support So You Get What You Need

How do you approach someone so that you get the support you need, and don't end up back in the blaming position, feeling more spent, or sucked into someone else's pain?

The answer: Be clear in your request as in these examples::

"I need to get clarity on an issue I am struggling with. Do you have a few minutes to listen while I just think out loud?"

"I would like to talk through an issue that I have been wrestling with. Can you be a sounding board for me as I sort my thoughts and feelings?"

"I am feeling really hurt and am having trouble thinking clearly about what happened at work today. Would you be willing to be my coach as I verbally brainstorm solutions?"

"I need feedback on how I came across in our team meeting today. Can you share your observations with me?"

If during the conversation you see that the person is not giving you appropriate support, here is what you can say to reorient or end the conversation:

"Thank you for your willingness to help me. However, I ask that you just listen, rather than offer advice."

"I appreciate your concern, however, it would help me if you just hear me, rather than vent your own frustrations."

"I need you to ask questions to check my assumptions rather than expressing your opinions."

"Let's reschedule a time to talk when you are not so busy or distracted."

Find Support Within Yourself

In looking back over his journey to heal from a major betrayal, one of our clients said, "While external support was helpful, I didn't really move toward healing until I was able to support myself."

You, too, have an enormous capacity to support yourself. You even have the power to heal yourself, should you choose to. Healing

---

Momentary Stillness

Taking time to pause and create moments of stillness throughout your day supports your healing process. Doing so enables you to take stock of your condition and needs.

1. Take 60 seconds now and then to pause to connect with your body and your breath.
2. Deeply inhale and exhale. Bring your focus to the area of your body where you are feeling tension; painful or negative feelings tend to lodge themselves as tension spots in different parts of your body.
3. Breathe deeply into that area, visualizing the release of the layers of tightness and the knots of tension shrinking with each breath.

This centering practice is designed to give you pause, break built-up tension, and release negative emotions embedded in your body.

---

begins with your choice to listen to yourself and to an internal voice that says you deserve healing and renewal. When you take the time to be present, thoughtful, and purposeful, your energy begins to expand and you return to yourself.

Sometimes the greatest form of support you can give to yourself is stillness. Actually doing nothing may be exactly what you need most. Give yourself permission to step back to create space and distance. Doing so will provide perspective about what you are experiencing and what you may need from others.

Many people we have worked with find it helpful to engage in gentle movement, such as yoga, a walk, a light run, or easy swim that supports introspection and gets stagnant energy moving. Journaling is another powerful venue wherein you may provide yourself support. In journaling, there is both a release that lightens your mind and heart, and learning that moves you along the path of healing. The act of putting your thoughts and feelings on paper validates them; once you accept them as written, you open part of yourself to hear the insight that is within you but may be blocked or buried in your pain.

Here, for instance, are a few insights from Dennis's journal, written in the middle of the night as he lay in a hospital bed during his second bout with cancer:

"In stillness, we can listen to our inner being: who we are and what we need. Stillness is the window to our soul."

"Pain is a great teacher. Many lessons lie in its presence; that is, if we are still enough to listen and learn."

"In stillness, we can connect with that part of us which knows how to heal ourselves, that part of us that knows the core truth, our truth: of who we are, of what we need to learn and grow and accomplish our life's purpose and destiny."

Dennis learned through journaling that in the space of stillness, with his doubt and fear quieted, he was able to give himself the kind of support that no one else could give. He was able to connect with his Higher Self for strength and comfort.

Reflection Question
Where is your place of stillness?

Use Journaling to Support Yourself

Rebuilding trust is a process of inquiry. Your questions guide the journey. In your journal, write down what comes to mind as you consider these questions:

? What happened?

Why is this situation hitting me so hard?

Why am I feeling vulnerable?

What is this situation/pain telling me?

What do I need?

What do I need to tell someone else about?

What knocked me off my feet?

What is making me feel uncomfortable?

>> **Trust Tip**   *Some of our greatest insight can come through stillness with ourselves and by talking about our insights with others.*

When You Have Been Betrayed

A global organization laid-off employees company-wide due to a downturn in the domestic market. Gail, Karl, and Dawn, old friends who worked in different areas of the business, were laid off on exactly the same day.

    Feeling betrayed by her boss, the company, and the situation, Gail reached out for support. She spoke with friends and colleagues and sought help from trained counselors to work through her pain. In the mornings she wrote her difficult thoughts in a journal, and in the evenings she worked out her negative feelings at the gym. She took responsibility for herself in the situation and, as a result, has moved through her pain to excel in new opportunities.

    Karl reached out to his managers for support, but they refused to give it to him because they said if they helped him, they would have to help fifteen others as well. Not having time for all of them and not wanting to show favoritism, they suggested Karl talk to family and friends outside of the company. Karl found that they didn't know how to help, and so their support was inadequate, especially now that he felt doubly betrayed by his managers. He had given so much of himself to the job prior to the layoff and had been a consistent high performer. With that resume, he moved quickly into new job with long hours, but it is less than satisfactory. Devastated and feeling victimized, Karl directs his anger toward his former managers. He remains stuck in his anger and has not been able to process his feelings or move on successfully.

    Dawn did not seek support at all. Instead, she buried her feelings and declined any assistance that was offered by her managers, HR, and even her friends and family. Saying she needed to concentrate on getting a new job, she dropped out of her cycling group, gained weight,

---

When You Have Been Hurt:
What You Can Expect from Support

Support means different things to different people and different situations require different kinds of support. It may not always feel like gentle handholding; sometimes it will be more like "tough love" that helps you to reframe the experience and take responsibility.

When you have been hurt, support can come in the form of:

- A **colleague** "lending a compassionate ear" as you express your pain
- Your **best friend** "holding up a mirror" so that you can face the truth honestly, even when you don't want to hear it
- A **life partner** giving you a "good, swift, verbal kick in the butt" and holding you accountable for your actions
- A **boss** coaching you to stop a negative pattern of minor betrayals to which you contribute
- A **coach** who helps you to redirect your energy and shift from wallowing in your feelings to looking at the bigger picture and the potential opportunities

---

and began experiencing back pain. She continued to blame others for her misfortune and not take the time to deal with her anger. To this day she is resentful of the circumstances and struggling with her unresolved feelings. She consults to former clients on a project-by-project basis but has not found a full-time job.

The three friends experienced such different outcomes. What was the key difference in their approaches? Gail successfully reached out to others and within herself for support, while neither Karl nor Dawn found support from others or from within themselves. Gail has reached a sense of peace in her life while both Karl and Dawn wrestle with the shadow of the past.

We cannot overstate how important it is for you to find the kind of support that is right for you. Whether your support is a professional, friend, family member, or colleague, share your feelings with a "trusted adviser." If you are dealing with a major betrayal, have him or her assist you in reconnecting with painful feelings from your past that are related to your present circumstance. Use this support to help you confront feelings of helplessness, hopelessness, or powerlessness so that you may reestablish your self-esteem and return to a fuller sense of self. Have the person help you to see the choices and options available to you.

When You Have Betrayed Others

When you realize that you have breached someone's trust, you have feelings, too. But it is less likely that someone will approach you, someone who hurt another, to see if you need support—especially if you are the boss or supervisor. Yet you, too, are human and deserve support.

You will have to go through the same Steps for healing as the person who was betrayed because you are hurting, too. Sometimes the realization that you have hurt another person can cause deeper discomfort than when you are the one who has been hurt by someone else. The betrayal of the self is a deeply felt betrayal. You need support to provide you with perspectives that you may not be able to see through your pain and guilt. Support will help you to regain your confidence and be able to be fully present with the person you betrayed in order to heal that relationship.

You first need to give yourself support so that you are able to observe the situation and fully acknowledge the impact of your behavior on the other person. You also need support to work through your own feelings of vulnerability, shame, embarrassment, or blame. Support will help you to see that, while you may have lost your footing, you are not a "bad" person.

Here's an example of how someone might transition from observation, impact, and surfacing feelings to asking specific questions for support:

> *"I hurt someone else and I am ashamed, embarrassed, and feeling guilty. As a result, the other person has shunned me and I feel isolated and abandoned."*

When You Have Hurt Someone: What You Can Expect from Support

You may think that the only kind of support you "deserve" when you've hurt someone else is "tough love" that helps you take responsibility and figure out how to avoid making the same mistake again. But you need more than that. You also need a sounding board, compassion, and a place to express your feelings.

A support conversation could sound something like this:

Jorge: *I heard what happened in the meeting. You're getting pretty beaten up for your mistake. How are you doing?*

Carlos: *I feel awful. I can't believe what I have done. How could I be so thoughtless? I just want to crawl in a hole and hide.*

Jorge: *I won't say anything to anyone else. You can let it out with me.*

Carlos: *I am so ashamed of myself. I feel embarrassed and guilty.*

Jorge: *What can I do to help you right now?*

Carlos: *I just need someone to talk to, someone who will listen without judging, blaming, or criticizing me. Someone who will help me to sort out my thinking and allow me to express my feelings.*

Jorge: *I am here for you Carlos. Use me for whatever you need.*

Carlos: *Thanks. I knew I could count on you to be there for me.*

"I made a mistake and I feel like hell. I want to understand what caused me to behave in such a way. How did I lose my footing?"

"I want to know if I should be beating myself up so much for my blunder. How do I make this better? How do I give restitution to the person I hurt?"

"How do I get the relationship back? How do I make this pain go away?"

When you are ready to seek support, it is best that you not go to the person you hurt or individuals closely aligned with that person.

Your support person needs to be present with you and detached from what happened. It is almost impossible for people close to the situation to overcome their own hurt feelings to be an objective source of support for you.

When You Want to Help Others Rebuild Trust

Ralph thought he was next in line for the director's job. He had worked his way up through the ranks diligently for the last twelve years and had a good working relationship with his board of directors, who were aware of his big plans to take the agency to new heights.

When Ralph didn't get the job, he was awestruck and devastated. "How could that be? I don't believe it!" he repeated again and again to himself and to his wife, Carol. Carol supported Ralph by listening, reflecting, and helping him to surface his feelings. She offered him solace and compassion. But when Ralph started to blame others for his misery, she put her foot down. "Stop your bellyaching and wallowing in self-pity. Take some responsibility for yourself!"

Carol challenged Ralph to look beyond his pain. She encouraged him to see both the positive and negative truth of the situation, which he was unwilling to face. Through her support, Ralph was able to reframe his situation, and shift from trying to preserve his pride and ego to exploring the choices and opportunities now available to him.

Just as getting support for yourself takes many forms, giving support may take many forms as well. Even as you support one person, your role, like Carol's in the story above, may shift from being a quiet sounding board to actively challenging the person's assumptions. Take a look at "When You Want to Help Others" sections throughout the book. They contain the nuts and bolts of providing support for each Step in the healing process. We provide guidance specific to each Step within each of those chapters, and you will notice that the support you offer will often circle back to prior Steps.

In addition to understanding the trajectory of the Seven Steps for Healing, there are some basic skills that are fundamental to providing support, no matter the phase of the healing process. We provide a primer on three of these fundamentals here for you to use in each of the other Steps.

Maintain Clear Intentions

Before supporting someone else, you need to make sure you are emotionally ready and clear in your intentions. Use this checklist to know that you are prepared:

- Are you aware of any of your feelings that might get in the way of supporting another effectively? Are you feeling blame or anger because you were let down? Are you able to see beyond these feelings?

- Can you take on the mind-set of a learner—someone curious enough to want to know more in order to create more capacity for healing? Or are you in judging mode, willing to jump to conclusions without testing your assumptions?

- Are you open to challenging some of your own assumptions regarding the situation? It is important that you do not bring in your own baggage; doing so will compromise the situation.

- Are you clear that your "job" is supporting the other person in working through his or her feelings? You are not there to "fix" or solve the problem. Your job is to allow *him* to do *his* work.

Listen

"I know my boss, Nigel, cares because he really listens to me. He hears me, sees my vulnerability. Being in this place helps me to accomplish A LOT! Being able to talk issues through with him has helped me to get through the worst year of my life because of my painful divorce."

Listening is a powerful source of support. When people are in pain they need to tell their story and be heard. Earlier, we wrote

Supportive Listening

Listening is a fundamental skill that is essential for supporting others. Many people think it's as easy as being quiet, but it's not that simple. Listening involves tuning into verbal and nonverbal information, hearing the message, and communicating your understanding.

Assess your supportive listening behaviors by asking yourself these questions:

? Are you willing to listen fully to another's feelings and frustrations, even when he or she may get intense?

Are you able to demonstrate genuine concern and empathy when you listen?

Are you able to hear not only others' words, but also to pick up on the subtle, non-verbal cues they are giving?

Do you ask questions to clarify the other's point of view?

Do you actively reflect and summarize others' comments to ensure understanding?

Do you avoid interrupting the other person before she is done speaking?

Do you listen more than you talk to the other person?

Are you able to keep your mind from wandering so that you never fail to hear what is said?

Do you ask questions rather than offer solutions?

Do you tend to understand what the other is saying, so that he doesn't need to correct you?

Do you truly listen to what is being said instead of using mental energy to consider your responses?

Supportive listening is more than a skillful behavior. It takes genuine compassion to "be there" for another and assist her in "doing her work." When you do so in an authentic way, you not only support the other person, you serve your Higher Self.

about how you can support your own healing by being still and present to yourself through meditation, journaling, and exercise. You can also extend your calm presence to those you want to help. Sometimes

---

Tips for Giving Support

What do you do and say in a support-giving conversation, especially when the person you're trying to help is stuck in her pain or blind to other perspectives? Support conversations are complex and no "cheat sheet" can adequately address sensitive human emotions. The following tips from our colleague, Rob Goldberg, are intended to help guide you, but not to replace your true compassion and empathy, which are more important than any single technique.

What You Can Do

- Temporarily stop trying to work on solutions. Shift the agenda to focus on the individual's feelings. Notice nonverbal behavior.

- Hear the person out; listen deeply and ask for more information.

- Validate and acknowledge her feelings in your own words. Summarize to ensure she experiences being fully heard.

- Ask about other issues. Don't be satisfied that the first topic mentioned is the key driver of her feelings.

- Postpone the conversation to a time when the individual is ready, or agree to stop, if his feelings become too intense for you to handle comfortably.

- Ensure that the rescheduled conversation does indeed take place or support her to find more appropriate options for support.

What You Might Say

"You seem upset; tell me about it."

"You don't seem ready to talk about the topic. I notice that you are more quiet than usual."

"I'm hearing your frustration."

"You don't seem able to put yourself in the picture right now; rather, I hear you mostly blaming other people. I'd like to understand better."

"What can you do to get beyond these negative feelings?"

---

support can be as simple as sitting down over a beverage with a colleague who is going through a tough time and being present to her story. You support others as you listen while they share their concerns, fears, and anxieties. Create or seize informal opportunities to have them talk through their concerns.

Help Solutions Rise to the Surface

To best help others, support them in coming up with their own solutions instead of providing the solutions. The Golden Rule here: Ask, don't tell. The power is asking the right questions to help them discover solutions for themselves.

Ask, don't tell

As you help someone move through the next four Steps of the healing process, try supportive questions such as these:

"Tell me what you think would help the situation."

"If you were the other person, how might you see the situation?"

"What do you think the person you hurt might need you to understand and acknowledge most? How can you do that?"

"In what ways can you demonstrate that you understand the impact of your behavior?"

"What is stopping you from reaching out to the other person?"

Through the deliberate acts of giving support, you express your own trustworthiness, and you participate in trust begetting trust. You amplify your own healing—whether that healing was last week or ten years ago, and whether it was at work or home, for the benefit of others, your teams, or your organization. You help create a workplace where trust can be rebuilt again and again.

Reframe
the Experience

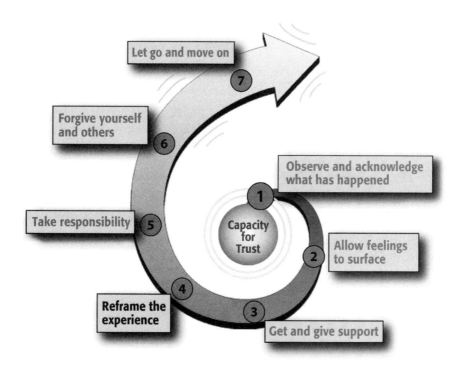

"You are in charge of your own attitude—whatever others do or circumstances you face. The only person you can control is yourself."

—Marian Wright Edelman
Founder and President of Children's
Defense Fund

Step Four is a turning point in your healing. With compassion as your partner, you reframe the situation from pain to gain by seeing the bigger picture surrounding the event, focusing on your choices and opportunities, and identifying the lessons you can learn. The gifts that come from healing are within your reach.

Reframing your perspective on a breach of trust—whether you were hurt or hurt someone else—can help you to see the greater purpose of this experience in your life.

It is as if you are on an archeological dig, only this is an exploration within yourself. You'll go deep inside to seek wisdom through genuine inquiry. Through reframing, you are able to transform your experience of loss, fear, or vulnerability to a rite of passage. You will be able to use the hurt and pain as stepping-stones to professional and personal growth and renewal. Whether the betrayal was intentional or unintentional, you learn to listen to and trust in your Higher Self. You develop an understanding and respect for relationships and your trustworthiness deepens, allowing you to have a greater and deeper influence on others and on your workplace.

Depending on the intensity of the situation and "which side" you are on, you may be able to reframe a situation right away, or it may take time to develop a deeper level of understanding. Over time—days, weeks, perhaps months or years—you will experience waves, or deeper layers, of understanding about relationships, life, and of yourself. All in all, reframing revolves around answering the core questions in the box.

> *"Our greatest glory is not in never falling, but in rising every time we fall."*
> —Confucius

See the Bigger Picture

We know it may be hard for you to see beyond your pain. A person who was badly hurt once said to us, "You've got to be kidding. There is no bigger picture that would explain this behavior." His

Questions to Help Reframe Your Experience

Healing is a journey of inquiry, and reframing relies on asking questions. Reflecting on the reframing questions here will help you to sort out your thoughts and emotions, make meaning out of what you experienced, and arrive at greater insight.

Take yourself to a place of stillness to quiet your anxiety, frustration, or fears. With compassion as your partner, remain open to the opportunity to learn and remain optimistic that you will be served by considering:

? Why did this happen?

What extenuating circumstances might be at play? Is there something I may not be aware of?

What options do I have for responding differently?

What can I take from this experience?

What lessons do I need to learn?

What is the purpose of this event in my life at this point?

response is quite understandable. We encouraged him—and we encourage you—to look in three directions to gain a broader perspective: beyond yourself, into the other person's experience, and within yourself.

Beyond Yourself

Compare your situation to what may be happening to others within your division, organization, industry, or community. No matter

No matter how bad you have it, someone else has it worse.

how bad you have it, someone else has it worse. Have your hours been cut? Think of those who have lost their jobs entirely. Did a co-worker not deliver his part of the project this time? Consider that there are people in your position in other divisions who never have help on a project. Did you learn of your company's merger by reading about it in the newspaper? Ask yourself if your management might have been contractually required to keep quiet, or if they even knew that the news was going to hit the paper. Perhaps they were as caught off-guard as you were.

 Reflection Question

How might you reframe a situation you are currently facing?

Into the Other Person's Experience

Seek to learn what might have been going on for the other person or people involved in the situation. In this way, you reframe with compassion and begin the forgiveness that is in Step Six. Many factors contribute to why people behave the way they do. That's why it is important to come from a place of compassion to understand the bigger picture and extenuating circumstances, whether you are seeking to understand why someone betrayed you or why someone reacted so intensely to your behavior. Ask what might have been going on for the other person that caused him or her to act or react in this way.

> **?** Was she under pressure, trying to meet unrealistic deadlines and feeling pushed up against the wall?
>
> Was he under stress because he was up all night with a sick child?
>
> Is she worried that she may lose her job and therefore feeling afraid?
>
> Was he hurting, in pain, and acting in a state of confusion?
>
> Did she strike out at you in an attempt to protect herself?

Putting yourself in someone else's shoes allows you to understand extenuating circumstances. Doing so allows you to develop

Seeing an Even Bigger Picture

When you struggle to see beyond yourself, look to your personal life for a reference point for reframing. We have all experienced letdowns of one kind or another.

Let's look at one such experience in Dennis's life:

In 1971, Dennis was a junior in college. He went into the hospital to have corrective surgery for a broken nose. Since Dennis's family received healthcare from the military, Dennis's operation was scheduled at Philadelphia Naval Hospital. Complications with his recovery, including acute maxillary sinusitis bordering on cerebral meningitis, kept him in the hospital beyond the anticipated recovery time. He spent his twenty-first birthday with his face so puffed-up from the infection that his eyes were swollen shut. Dennis lay all alone in the hospital ward, feeling sorry for himself.

Then the next morning, a huge military transport plane landed on the base. The ward filled with wounded soldiers from Vietnam. Dennis saw guys his age and younger who were missing arms, legs, and other body parts. Some even had parts of their faces blown off.

It struck Dennis quite profoundly that his illness was a temporary condition, but many of these young soldiers were permanently marred and disfigured. Dennis realized he had it good. Those other guys were the ones who should feel sorry for themselves.

Yet, for the most part, the opposite was true. As he got to know them, Dennis learned that they felt like the lucky ones. They were still alive and happy to be home, while their buddies were still being shot and killed in jungles and rice paddies on the other side of the world.

Dennis had an opportunity to reframe the entire experience when the bigger perspective of war and life-long disability presented itself. He realized that it had been very easy for him to get caught up in his own challenges and feel "victimized" by the circumstances. He also realized that as bad as you think you have it, someone else has it worse. You see, it is always a matter of perspective. You choose the outlook you adopt.

compassion for others involved. One of our clients, Larry, was able to reframe a situation with just such compassion:

> *Larry felt very let down. Over the last six months, he had noticed that Vicki, previously his strongest player, wasn't performing well. He spoke with her repeatedly about missed deadlines. In each conversation, she promised to do better. When she didn't improve, Larry met with Vicki.*
>
> *"Please help me to understand what is contributing to this slippage in your performance. I don't want to take disciplinary steps, but I am afraid that it's getting to the point that I have no choice."*
>
> *Overcome by humiliation, Vicki mustered the courage to tell Larry that she had been suffering from depression. She let him know that this condition made it difficult for her to concentrate and impacted her productivity. She explained that she had been too embarrassed to tell him.*
>
> *With this broader perspective, Larry let Vicki know that he understood what she was going through: His wife suffered from bouts of depression. He was able to shift from considering disciplinary steps to offering compassionate measures to equip Vicki with work arrangements that supported her treatment path. Over time, Vicki returned to her previous level of high performance.*

Within Yourself

Next, consider what else might have been going on for you that could have contributed to your behavior or reaction to a situation.

? What caused you to act in such a way?

Were you overtired, stressed-out, rushing, or pushing?

Were you over-reacting because the pain from unresolved past hurts was surfacing?

Were you yourself feeling betrayed and acting out of self-defense?

Were you feeling ganged-up on and responding out of fear?

Were you feeling vulnerable?

Looking at your broader experience helps you to put the situation into proper perspective. You extend compassion to yourself when you allow yourself to see that you were in a space of fear or vulnerability and lost your footing. You can then shift from beating yourself up to understanding yourself. You allow yourself to be human, and become prepared to take responsibility for your learning and address your vulnerability in Step Five.

"We don't see things as they are. We see things as we are."

—Anais Nin
Novelist and diarist

Focus on Choices and Opportunities

Bad things happen to people all the time. It's not what happens to you that really counts; it's what you *choose* to do about it that makes a difference. One of our clients came to realize that when he exercises choice, he opens up a "vast field of opportunities and possibilities" that were not available to him when he was stuck in the victim mode.

What you focus on will determine your outcomes. Focus on the damage that was done and live in the past, or focus on the positive possibilities and opportunities and move forward. When you change your attitude, you change your life.

"Pain is inevitable; suffering is optional."

—Anonymous

Identify the Lessons

The challenges you face, the mistakes you make, and the patterns you repeat provide you with the lessons you need to learn. We have found that the more an individual resists a situation and the related lessons, the more the situation works against him or her.

Where Is Your Focus?
On the Obstacle or the Opportunity?

Earl Nightingale, the late motivational speaker, once said, "The mind moves in the direction of our currently dominant thought." Keep that in mind and consider these questions to help you reframe obstacles as opportunities:

? What are your current dominant thoughts about the challenges you have or are currently experiencing? Are they on what is working, or what is not working?

Where is your focus? Is it on what was lost or what can be gained?

Are you concentrating your efforts on pointing the finger and blaming, or on seeking to understand?

Are you criticizing and judging the other person, or extending compassion? Are you invested in making her wrong, so you get to be right? If so, what does that stance get you?

Are you able to take action? If not, why not? What or who is keeping you stuck?

In what direction are you choosing to move? What will it take to make the shift?

How aware are you of the thoughts that are running or creating your life?

Often, a pattern will repeat itself again and again until you pay attention. Acknowledging what you have learned through a situation, as painful as the situation may be, supports healing.

We all have struggles in relationships; they come in different shapes and sizes, at different times, and in various timeframes. Sometimes the lessons can appear and be applied even before significant damage is done to the relationship:

Michelle recently began working with a new client, Mike. Michelle's role was to provide support to Mike as he worked to address the accu-

mulated effect of patterns of trust-breaking behavior that were dramatically impacting his team's performance. His organization was in an acute state of pain.

As she arrived for her second visit, she felt a shift in Mike. The warmth, receptivity, and easiness she had experienced with him at her initial visit were replaced with distance and seeming aloofness. Michelle was disturbed and internally wondered, "What is going on here: Has there been a shift in his interest?"

Before she moved too far down the road of doubt, Michelle collected herself and asked a question. "Mike, is there something going on that I don't know about? Is there anything troubling you that would be helpful for me to know?"

Mike responded candidly and with frustration, "Now that you ask, yes, there is. I have tried to reach you for the last two days and am deeply disturbed that you have not returned my phone calls. If I can't reach you, I question to what extent we can be successful making movement here."

Mike also shared that he perceived that Michelle was too busy and had "more important" clients. He needed to know that his team counted and would have her attention. Michelle felt like a deer caught in the headlights; she had no knowledge of his calls. She acknowledged his frustration and shared his alarm. They then did some quick trouble-shooting, which helped Michelle discover a malfunction in her cell phone voicemail delivery system that had caused messages to be delayed.

On the surface, this may sound like a rather insignificant incident. However, its very simplicity highlights how such breakdowns create doubt. As Michelle and Mike were able to move through this breakdown in a matter of minutes, it provided perspective and a reference point that built further trust in their relationship.

Together, they recognized how quickly assumptions can impact perceptions and how important it is to check them out. Mike learned

What Lessons Can You Learn?

Reflect on the following questions to support you in learning from your challenges:

[?] What can you learn from the situation you are now facing?

What lessons need to be gained?

How can you benefit from these circumstances?

What meaning and purpose does this challenge provide you?

---

that he could bring a concern to Michelle's attention and that she was willing to listen. Michelle knew that Mike was able to hear a broader perspective and that he did not need to be "right." She recognized how vulnerable he was feeling and how the state of his organization was coloring his reaction. She saw signs that he needed compassion. They were both reminded of the lessons to challenge assumptions, to seek understanding before affixing blame, and to articulate and address frustrations before they cause a breakdown in a relationship.

On a more practical level, Michelle discovered a glitch in her new cell phone carrier's voicemail system that needed to be fixed.

Sometimes you may find yourself stuck in challenges and unable to see lessons. Emotions and feelings of frustration continue to rise to the surface and you just can't seem to move past them. You may wonder, "What is my problem? Why can't I get past this?"

We have found that when people are stuck in finding the lessons inherent in the situation, one of two dynamics is often at play. There may be another element of what happened that needs to be more fully acknowledged. Or, it may be that the current event has triggered memories of past experiences that weren't fully healed. In either case, reaching out for support will bring you nurturing compassion that can help you shift from seeing obstacles and looking at what was not or what has been lost, to opportunity and what has been gained. You reframe when you look for that greater purpose.

When You Have Been Betrayed

When you have been hurt, start reframing by gaining a broader perspective. As painful as your situation may be, it is unlikely to be "life and death." Remind yourself of people who have it worse. Take some time to gather some facts around the event. We worked with one department in which employees felt betrayed by a new supervisor's unfair "decision" to allow only some "favored" employees to telecommute. When they finally asked the supervisor about it, he answered that he had inherited these situations and he was very open to extending them to others in the department if they asked. The employees' assumptions had simply been wrong.

Take a look at Jo Ellen's story to learn more about the destructive power of assumptions:

Jo Ellen's boss did not select her for a promotion. Instead, she brought in someone from outside the organization for the new Operations Director role. Jo Ellen was hurt, but, because of her pride and at the risk of feeling incompetent, she never asked her boss why she was not chosen for the director's job. She assumed that her boss didn't value her contribution or have confidence in her abilities.

Because she had to work with the new Operations Director, Jo Ellen just decided to push on. She tried to improve her skills in her current role while she buried her feelings, and felt wronged and sorry for herself. She distanced herself from her boss who once was a close friend and confidant.

Three years passed. While in a performance review session with her boss and the Operations Director, they both acknowledged how much Jo Ellen had grown professionally in her role, particularly in the area of executive coaching. They recognized her increased value and contribution to the organization.

At that moment, Jo Ellen realized that not getting that director's position was probably the best thing that could have happened to her at that time. She now understood that if she had been consumed with managing day-to-day operations, she would not have been able to improve and hone her coaching skills as she had done. She was able to reframe the situation: In her enhanced position, she had been able to make a greater contribution to the organization and develop a specific and valuable skill.

Afterward, her boss approached her and shared how much she missed their formerly close relationship. Surprised and moved, Jo Ellen shared similar sentiments of the loss she experienced.

As you can see from Jo Ellen's story, you can focus on the obstacles and the loss by choosing to play the victim and remain hurt, wronged, and feeling sorry for yourself. Or, you can choose to see the opportunity by working through the pain of disappointment and frustration, or of feeling wounded and misunderstood.

Jo Ellen was finally able to reframe, and in that moment was able to see the cost of her victimhood. By not checking out her assumptions, she had lost the close relationship with her boss for over three years.

When we share with our clients the concept that you can choose to work through the pain of disappointment, frustration, hurt, or of feeling wronged and misunderstood, a number often respond, "But you don't really understand. *I* was wronged. *I* was betrayed. *I* hurt and I *deserve* to get back and get even."

The unarticulated underlying statement is, "Because I was wronged, I have a right to feel helpless and victimized. I have a right to wallow in my self-pity." Some people remain victims for days, months, and even years. Their attitude is fraught with frustration, irritation, and disappointment. They are attached to making others wrong.

Others choose to work through the pain by releasing the hurtful feelings in constructive ways, with an open, optimistic, and positive outlook. They learn powerful lessons about themselves and grow through the process. Jo Ellen learned that she tended to focus on the negatives rather than the positives, and that everything has a purpose, even though she may not understand or realize it until long after the event has occurred.

When You Have Betrayed Others

> *"You learn more from losing than you do with winning."*
> —John McEnroe
> Former No. 1 World Professional
> Tennis Player

If you have betrayed another, a big part of reframing is thinking about what else was going on for you. For instance, if you yourself were feeling betrayed, you were more likely to betray another. Being hurt gives you a feeling of "validation" to betray another: "Because they betrayed me, I feel justified in betraying them back." In that space, you are less likely to listen to your better judgment. Then, you are likely to betray yourself by acting in ways inconsistent with your values and who you are.

Let's look back at the story of Kerri and Kim that we introduced in Step One. Kim felt betrayed by Kerri, her boss, who had taken on consulting assignments while on an extended medical leave. In coming to terms with what she had done, Kerri began to understand that she had behaved in the very way her boss had behaved toward her. She had felt used and taken advantage of by him, so she used and took advantage of him in return. She lied about not being well enough to return to work while, at the very same time, she was working elsewhere. She lost sight of the impact of her choice on her team.

Through these actions, Kerri betrayed not only her team, but also herself. In her own pain, she lost herself and what she stood for. Betrayal of self, whether in reaction to being betrayed or as an outcome of being under severe stress, is often at the root of betraying behavior.

Kerri's situation shows that in reviewing your role in a hurtful situation, it may be helpful to look deeper, beyond the surface of this one experience, and observe whether you were repeating a pattern. Are there similar themes in the nature of the trust-breaking mistakes you make? What lessons can you learn about yourself? Does the following admission from one of our clients resonate with you?

> *"I can't tell you how many times I have made mistakes and ended up hurting others and myself due to my rushing to do too much in too little time, pushing to meet unrealistic deadlines. I have repeated this painful lesson throughout my life and it has cost me, and those around me, way too much. Through my thoughtlessness and carelessness, I have deeply hurt others and myself."*

In taking stock of the times you may have hurt others out of carelessness or mistakes you made while rushing, you may begin to see patterns that lead to broad lessons. For Michelle, this lesson of pushing too hard to achieve a goal at the cost of pain to herself and others around her gave her life much, much more than the benefit of achieving one specific goal.

As you become more aware of the patterns of these challenges and the lessons they are trying to teach, you are able to approach challenges and work through them more purposefully because each has deeper meaning in the context of your life. They may or may not be easier to deal with. However, over time, you become more able to embrace these challenges with less fear and resistance. Instead you will approach them with more curiosity and wonderment.

 Reflection Question

What patterns do you repeat in life that hurt others and yourself?

Learning Lessons from Your Mistakes

To support yourself in reframing the situation when you have betrayed another or yourself and in gaining the lessons to be learned, ask yourself questions such as:

? What are the deeper lessons that I need to learn from these experiences?

What lessons haven't I grasped fully?

What still needs to be worked on?

What have been the major issues that I have encountered?

What kinds of people keep on showing up in my life, presenting problems to me?

What is the universe trying to tell me that I am not "getting" or need to work through?

Once you understand your patterns and have raised your awareness, you are better able to "step up to the plate" for your next challenge or assignment with greater preparedness. Through insight, you will make different choices, ones that are more in relationship with who you are and how you want to bring yourself to others.

When You Want to Help Others Rebuild Trust

Your first step to help someone reframe a situation is to *clarify your intentions*. Be aware of your own needs that might taint or get in the way of you effectively coaching another.

When you give support, you are creating a sacred space for healing. You build a safe container through your compassion and personal experience. By referencing situations, perspectives, and lessons beyond the scope of the situation at hand, you give the other person options for reframing. At the same time, you're likely to learn even more about your own experience as you apply the lessons you learned to someone else's situation.

Assignments to Help Another Reframe

Here are some examples of assignments you can give to others to help them reframe and take responsibility:

- Ask questions to learn more about the context surrounding the situation.
- Find a time to ask the other person involved for her perspective on the situation.
- In your journal, reflect upon the answers to one of the reframing questions listed here.
- Make a list of what you could have done differently in the situation.
- Ask someone who knows you well if he knows if you have ever experienced a similar situation or acted in a similar fashion in another context.

Remember that before the person you are supporting can reframe the situation, he needs go through the first three Steps for Healing. It is only after he has effectively engaged those three Steps that he is able to receive probing about the possibilities and opportunities that the challenge may provide.

At that point, you can help the individual by *asking questions*. You can use the questions for reframing that were listed earlier in this chapter to help guide your discussions. When people are stuck or in pain, they cannot see that which may be clear to you.

> *When people are stuck or in pain, they cannot see that which may be clear to you.*

Sometimes, helping someone to see his options and gain perspective involves *giving assignments*. We often give assignments to our executive coaching clients, to support them in shifting from feeling at the mercy of changing circumstances (whether they are internal to the organization, such as challenging employee dynamics, or external, such as shifting market conditions). These assignments help leaders to reframe their perspective so they can actively take responsibility in the situation.

> **» Trust Tip** *Healing is a process of inquiry. Reflecting on reframing questions helps us to understand the context of the betrayal or loss, and to sort out our thoughts and feelings regarding the experience.*

You can help others learn to reframe tough situations at work, such as moving through change, dealing with restructuring, or working through betrayal, by giving assignments that break the big healing process into manageable chunks. Be sure to follow up to see what creative ideas the person you are helping came up with and what support he or she needs in moving forward to implement the ideas.

Remember also to recognize the work it takes to complete these assignments, as well as other aspects of the healing process. When you acknowledge a colleague's efforts to reframe an experience, you validate his decision to move from being a victim to making a conscious choice to heal. You help him celebrate his return from his deep plunge within himself. Encourage him to give thanks for what he has, and then ask for what he wants. In leading that articulation, you help to create the energy needed to make the shift away from pain.

Take Responsibility

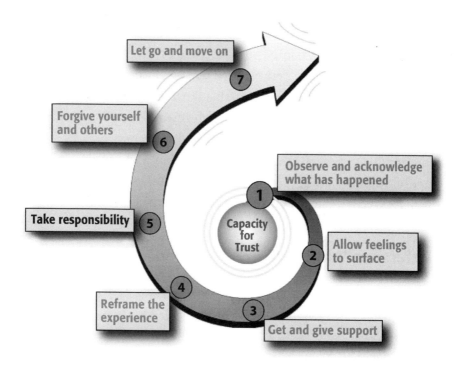

Let go and move on

7

Forgive yourself
and others

6

Observe and acknowledge
what has happened

1

Take responsibility 5

Capacity
for
Trust

Allow feelings
to surface

2

4

Reframe the
experience

3

Get and give support

"The price of greatness is responsibility."

—Sir Winston Churchill
British Prime Minister and statesman

Courage is your partner as you take responsibility for your role in broken trust, because telling yourself and others the impeccable truth without exceptions, justifications, or rationalizations is very tough. Telling the truth is the fundamental basis for trust in all relationships, including those at work. By telling the truth, you begin to take responsibility and acknowledge your mistakes.

> *Telling the truth is the fundamental basis for trust in all relationships.*

You may find that you dip back into reframing (Step Four) and forward into forgiving yourself and others (Step Six) as you go further and further down this path of healing. Step Five works hand-in-hand with those two compassion-oriented Steps.

In any relationship between two people, both parties contribute to the dynamics that unfold, whether trust is being built or broken. Taking responsibility for your part of the breakdown of trust and the resulting impact on others means looking at your actions, reactions, and resulting choices. You do so by determining what part of the situation you own, taking action to move forward, and recognizing the gains you have made by choosing the path of healing.

Determine What Part You Own

> *"I am only responsible for my actions and reactions. I am not responsible for someone else's hurtful behavior or unresolved past issues. He needs to own his part and I need to take responsibility for mine and not make excuses for the mistakes I made that contributed to this situation."*

It's fairly easy to see how a person who betrayed another would take responsibility for actions that led to the hurtful situation. It's a little more complicated for the one who was hurt to take responsibility. In that case, the responsibility is not for the actions *per se*, but for putting herself in the position to be hurt and for choosing how to respond.

You may not always like your choices and therefore, consciously or unconsciously, choose not to exercise one. But you do have choices in any situation, even when you are hurting. You do not have control over how another person behaves, or how they respond to you; you do, however, always have control over how you *choose* to respond.

To explore what part of the experience you own, ask yourself the following questions:

? What role or part did I play in the breakdown?

What did I do or not do that contributed to the betrayal?

Am I owning or disowning my part of the experience?

Am I making excuses or diverting blame away from myself?

Is it possible that I did not clearly state my needs or set firm boundaries with the other person?

Do I have a need to make the other person wrong so I can be right?

How have I betrayed myself or the other person in the relationship?

What did my inner voice tell me?

Did I listen to it?

If not, why?

Take Action

"I am still struggling with what happened. But I also know that I don't need to stay stuck. I know things can be different. I want things to be different. Next time, I need to not take things so personally. I can't keep beating myself up like this.

But changing this perspective will take time. It's about defining a new set of beliefs and associated behaviors and fostering those behaviors into habits for myself. I guess it is a continuous improvement process, one step at a time."

In Step Four, as you reframed the situation, you saw that you had a choice about whether to heal and move on, or stay stuck. With compassion as your partner, you looked at the bigger picture and were curious about extenuating circumstances. You sought to understand and looked for presenting lessons.

Here, in Step Five, you take action on that choice. You are now shifting from observing, feeling, and thinking to action.

Ask yourself these questions to identify actions you can take to move forward:

? Which of my needs still need to be addressed?

What problem do I need to solve?

What information do I need and how can I get it?

What actions can I take now to take charge of the situation?

What conversations do I need to have?

What feedback do I need to provide?

What do I need to set straight?

Realize What You Gain

"While the pain I endured from this situation was profound, I now realize that I have grown so much from this experience. When it comes down to it, I see that I was repeating a pattern that I developed to protect myself a long, long time ago. Now that I understand that pattern and the impact it has on my relationships, I can catch myself before I make the same mistake again."

We've said many times already that betrayal can be a teacher and a gift if you let it be. Now, as you take responsibility, the gains you'll make through healing come to life. Whether you are the one who has been hurt or who has hurt another, you can grow from this experience. As you take responsibility, your confidence, commitment, and energy will return. How they return varies depend-

---

Stuck?

Getting stuck and struggling to take responsibility is a sign that there may be more that you need to acknowledge to yourself. If you're having trouble with this Step, ask yourself:

> **?** Where am I struggling or getting stuck?
>
> What more needs to be acknowledged?
>
> What permission do I need to give myself to allow additional feelings to surface?
>
> What fears do I need to address?
>
> What additional support do I need to give myself?

---

ing on your vantage point; specific sections follow here that will go into more detail.

These questions support you in realizing what you gain from taking responsibility:

> **?** What could I have done differently in this situation?
>
> What could I learn about myself and others from taking responsibility?
>
> What will I do differently if I'm in this situation again?

In taking responsibility, start with small steps in the right direction. These steps may not be perfect or lead to a full acknowledgment of what you own and what you can learn, but at least you are doing something and are moving in the direction of renewal. Healing takes disciplined action, particularly when you are dealing with the larger and more overwhelming challenges. Healing is like a "do-it-yourself" home project: It may not get done in a day or one weekend, and it may not look perfect to other people, but you (and maybe only you) will know the benefit of the inner work you have accomplished.

When You Have Been Betrayed

*"You don't just deal with adversity. You use it to propel
you forward."*

—Erik Weihenmayer
First blind person to summit Mt. Everest

Taking responsibility for your part in a situation, particularly one in which someone else hurt you, is extremely difficult, but absolutely necessary for healing and growth. When we first met Lloyd, he didn't think he could get over the pain of having been betrayed by a close colleague, let alone take responsibility for his part. In this section, we follow Lloyd as he finds the courage to do so.

Here's how the story starts:

Lloyd and Jim were two trusted colleagues who worked closely together in IT at an international aid foundation. Between them they had an unwritten "contract" that they would support and cover for each other on the job. But then Jim secretly competed against Lloyd for a position he had wanted for years. The implicit contract broke down, and so did their trust.

Determine What Part You Own

Begin taking responsibility by determining your role in the breach. Healing and growth require you to be accountable for your behavior and the choices you made that may have contributed to the betrayal—even though others may have been misguided or wrong. You must always consider what your part might have been. You may need to own how you put yourself into the place that allowed you to be betrayed, and you will always need to own your choice in how you responded.

You begin to come to terms with what is yours to own by asking and answering some direct questions about what you did, or where you were emotionally, at the time the other person hurt you.

After much self-reflection, here's how Lloyd responded to these questions:

? What role or part did I play in the process?

> *"I assumed that Jim was totally trustworthy and that he supported me going for that promotion."*

> *"I was so naïve that I didn't realize that he was vying for the same position."*

> *"I was so trusting that I shared with him all my ideas on how to correct the system problem, knowing that the solution was critical to my application for the job."*

> *"I didn't have a clue that Jim would take the ideas and methods resulting from our collaboration and claim them as his own without giving me any credit or attribution."*

? What did I do or not do that contributed to the betrayal?

> *"When I realized what Jim had done, I was shocked. I retreated as a victim and didn't speak up or take action soon enough."*

> *"In addition, I was dealing with health issues at home, so I was distracted."*

> *"I didn't represent my work appropriately to the boss when I had the opportunity. That choice allowed me to be taken advantage of."*

? Am I owning or disowning my part of the experience?

> *"Initially, I made excuses and blamed Jim for what he had done to me. I was angry, hurt, and extremely resentful."*

> *"I now realize that I did not clearly set firm boundaries with Jim regarding my expectations of him."*

> *"I did not update my understanding of his interest by asking him if he planned to apply for the job."*

The next piece you need to own is your *reaction* to being hurt. The opposite of owning your reaction is choosing to remain a victim. Feeling like a victim does nothing to improve your situation; in

fact, it makes you feel powerless and hopeless. When you are in pain, you tend to project your feelings onto others and abdicate
any responsibility regarding the situation.

*When you are in pain,
you tend to project your
feelings onto others.*

In short, you blame others for your position and your pain.

Take Action

After owning your part in the situation, the next step is taking action.
The first move will almost always be a decision to forgo the victim
posture in favor of forward momentum.

The core question in this phase of taking responsibility is:

? What actions can I now take to take charge of the
situation?

Lloyd answered with:

"I will be more cautious with Jim and safeguard my work."

*"If I have to work with Jim in the future, I will set clear
boundaries and lay out stringent working agreements before I
collaborate with him."*

*"I will present and promote my original work more vigorously
to key stakeholders in the organization."*

*"I will speak up more readily when I feel taken advantage of. I
will make sure that I get credit for that which is mine to claim."*

Realize What You Gain

Taking responsibility causes you to leverage your pain to understand
your underlying, self-limiting issues. When you back up that self-discovery with action, you move yourself to a new plateau of self-awareness, performance, and possibility. You are on the edge of renewal.
In that way, taking responsibility for your behavior can reframe a
betrayal into a life-transforming event.

Dennis, for instance, used a 1975 life-threatening accident and
a sense of abandonment to propel him to a new way of living and
through a Master's degree in holistic health. Dennis's gain was life-

Recognizing the Victim Posture versus the Responsible Approach

When you assume the role of a victim, you abdicate responsibility and actually betray yourself, so it's important to recognize if you're stuck in that role. Here's a quick checklist comparing the victim posture with the responsibility-taking approach.

Victim Posture	Responsible Approach
Feels entitled	Feels personally accountable
Apathetic	Takes initiative
Carries grudges	Constructively works through disagreements
Operates with hidden agendas	Open and transparent
Closed to new ideas	Curious and approachable
Acts out toward others	Treats people with respect
Goes through the motions	Empowers self and others
Engages in workarounds	Deals with people directly
Does not take any risks	Takes appropriate risks
Gossips about others	Speaks with good purpose
Makes judgments	Seeks to understand

long health, a new career, and most importantly, the knowledge that he can turn any negative situation into a positive benefit, no matter what happens to him.

Likewise, Lloyd gained perspective about his self-limiting behaviors that were getting in the way of his fully expressing himself at work.

❓ What have I gained by going through this experience?

> *"I recognize that I need to protect my project work and research appropriately so I don't put myself in a vulnerable position."*

> *"I know now that I need to stand up for myself."*

"I also realize that making Jim wrong so I could be right was not productive or helpful to him or to me. In fact, in doing so, I betrayed myself by giving away my power to him. I won't make that mistake again."

"From now on, I am going to listen to my inner voice when it tells me to be more cautious."

When You Have Betrayed Others

We are often inspired by the courage of our clients and the personal and professional growth they achieve through healing. In Step Two, we introduced you to one of these clients we called Nina for the purposes of this book. She had betrayed the confidence of a colleague, Ted, by telling his boss that he was applying for a job in a different division. We pick up her story as she reframes the experience and takes responsibility for having hurt another:

For several weeks, Nina tried to apologize to Ted but he continued to shun her. Nina was truly flattened by her shame and remorse. But at home she complained to her husband that Ted was "overreacting" and not forgiving her. At one point, her husband supported her by being very direct with her. "What you did was really wrong, Nina. Face it."

In response, Nina turned her attention from Ted's reaction to herself. Neither blaming Ted for his reaction nor beating herself up for her mistake were taking her forward. After much self-reflection, she came to realize that she had been feeling vulnerable in her new position. Sharing information had felt like power: She demonstrated to her boss how well connected she was. In so doing, she had betrayed herself and her genuine talent for building relationships.

As she began to take full responsibility for her action and for her underlying vulnerability, she stopped beating herself up for her mistake. She took action by reminding herself of her strengths. In this place, she was able to make a full apology to Ted for the first time. She acknowledged the full impact the violation had had on Ted and took full responsibility for her actions without any defensiveness.

*While she wasn't able to make a meaningful restitution to Ted, she
learned a lesson about boundaries that she has applied since. Every time
someone shares potentially sensitive information with her, Nina asks
very directly if it's OK to share it with others. In the twenty-five years
since she began that practice, Nina has never again violated a confidence.*

When you hurt another person, it is critical for you to own your
behavior. In so doing, you open the door to healing. You take responsibility
when you acknowledge your mistake first to yourself and
then to the other person. *Apology* is another word for the authentic
and complete acknowledgment you make to the person you hurt;
our tips for apology are included in the box. Making that apology
is the major action you need to take to come to terms with your
responsibility.

Before you can apologize to someone else, you first need to be
responsible to yourself, and to understand fully what you are apologizing
for. Without that understanding, the apology is empty and
superficial. Preparing to make an apology involves noticing any
defensiveness you may still have and checking to see if you betrayed
yourself by the hurtful actions you took.

Defensiveness will cloud the issue and impact the effectiveness of
your outreach to the person you betrayed. You must be able to be
totally present with the other person in order to make a full apology.
Nina had to first stop blaming Ted for his reaction and then stop
beating herself up before she was able to be present and responsible
enough to make an effective apology to Ted.

Self-betrayal occurs when you act against your core values. As you
prepare to apologize, be honest with yourself. Were you centered and
grounded, or were you acting out of fear or rushing? Nina was vulnerable
in her new role and in her desire to stand out; in that place,
she compromised one of her core values. When you behave outside
your values, you hurt yourself and others. If you can include in your
apology how you betrayed yourself, you will show your authentic
ownership of your actions and honor your integrity.

The Anatomy of Apology: Seven Steps for Healing

Use what you're learning about the Seven Steps to discover and offer a complete apology.

1. Observe and acknowledge what happened

In the apology, it is important to acknowledge the impact your actions had on other people, even if what you did was unintentional.

I gossiped about how you and Joe were spending lots of time together outside of work. I recognize now that by doing so I spread rumors that weren't true and that those rumors have hurt your professional reputation and may hold you back from opportunities.

2. Allow feelings to surface

Demonstrate that you are sensitive to the impact of your actions. Express your feelings of remorse for having hurt the person.

I see that you are angry and I have hurt you. I understand that I have betrayed your trust and I sense that you are worried about your career. I am very ashamed of what I did and I am very disappointed in myself.

3. Get and give support

Offer to help in any way you can.

I can imagine that you don't trust me anymore, but I am willing to listen to all you need to say to me.

4. Reframe the experience

Put the experience into a larger context. Share what else was going on for you by way of explanation, not as a defense.

"Action speaks louder than words but not nearly as often."

—Samuel Clemens (Mark Twain)

Often, three simple words—"I am sorry"—demonstrate taking responsibility and go a long way in rebuilding trust. But a true apology is more than words: you also need to take action to restore the relationship. As John Kador said in his book *Effective Apolo-*

I now see that I gossiped about you so that I would be accepted into the group. When I came to the department, I felt so lonely and isolated. That doesn't excuse my behavior: it's just that I see now why I did it.

5. Take responsibility

Own that which is yours to own and pay back more than was perceived to be taken away. Make full restitution.

I was totally out of line in telling others about what you did with your time. I'm going to go back to the group and say that I shared information I shouldn't have. I'll let them know that I didn't know that you were both taking the same certification class and that your relationship was only professional.

6. Ask for forgiveness

Find out what needs to be said or done for the person to forgive you, but do not expect him or her to do so.

Is there anything else I can do so that you can forgive me?

7. Let go and move on

Promise not to repeat the hurtful act, with them or anyone else. Share your understanding of the impact of your actions and the lessons you learned.

I promise never to share personal information about you again. I also know not to gossip about anyone or anything. I understand that it hurt others and also destroys my own trustworthiness.

gy, "Apology demands that we extend ourselves by actually doing something."[1]

As you think about what actions to take to help repair the relationship, remember to give back more than was perceived to be taken away. We like to say "Make Amends and Return with Dividends." Rebuilding trust does not simply mean giving back what was taken away. It means returning something more than was taken away.

What does this concept look like in practice?

- If you were late in delivering your report last time, deliver the report earlier than expected next time.

- If you took too much time for your part of the presentation in your last meeting, next time give your team members most of your allotted time.

- If you are perceived to micromanage an employee, give him a larger role or responsibility in a key project when appropriate.

In thinking about what you are going to do differently going forward so that you are less likely to hurt this person or others again, consider two lessons that many people learn from having hurt others:

- *Manage expectations.* Avoid future betrayals by keenly managing expectations. A second betrayal hurts exponentially more than the first. People want to know what they can expect of you and then they want to trust that you'll follow through. To sustain trust in your relationships: under-promise and over-deliver.

- *Keep your promises.* Be careful of what you promise and what you appear to promise. Don't make promises that you know you can't keep. As soon as you realize that you may not be able to keep your promises, be upfront and renegotiate.

The final part of taking responsibility is recognizing personal gains you make by doing so. For instance, when you, like Nina in the earlier example, shift from beating yourself up for hurting the other person to taking action to make amends, you shift from being powerless to powerful.

As your sense of personal power returns, so will your confidence. Instead of hanging your head in shame, you can give back more and hold your head high. You will once again feel committed to this and other relationships, and gain energy from knowing that you did the right thing by apologizing and taking responsibility through actions.

Here are some of the gains people have expressed to us after they have taken full responsibility for hurting another:

"I am a better collaborator because I check my assumptions."

"I am more trustworthy now because I know the pain of letting down another."

"I am a better team member because I have learned that when I am stressed, I need to slow down, take a moment to breathe and clearly assess the situation instead of pushing forward and making unnecessary mistakes."

"I am more responsible. When I feel I have to prove myself to others, I ask myself, 'Where is that feeling coming from? Is it fear? Pride? Lack of competence?'"

When you make a mistake that lets others down and take responsibility for it, you gain invaluable wisdom that pervades all aspects of your life.

When You Want to Help Others Rebuild Trust

"We must become the change we want to see."

—Mahatma Gandhi

The best thing you can do to help others take responsibility is to authentically practice the behaviors that you want others to practice. In other words, you have to *walk the talk*. Supporting someone in taking responsibility is more than having a toolbox of methods and techniques. Support in this Step relies on your presence; that is, how you genuinely *show up* in your interactions with others.

Think about how you feel when people you trust are not taking responsibility or owning their part of situations. How likely are you to take advice from them? Consider:

- The HR professional who admonishes you for bashing the company, yet incessantly gossips about co-workers behind their backs.

Inspire Others to Take Responsibility

Your way of being affects your trustworthiness, and therefore your effectiveness in helping others take responsibility. To inspire others to take responsibility:

- **Be present.** Trust yourself to say and do the right thing at the right time. As Larry Dressler, in his book *Standing in the Fire*, says, "It is a specific kind of presence that others experience as fully engaged, open, authentic, relaxed, and grounded in purpose."[2]
- **Be giving.** Come from a desire to help and serve the other versus being self-serving in your intentions.
- **Be proactive.** Take actions to rebound from setbacks and adversity. Continue moving forward, rather than being reactive and retreating into despair.
- **Be accountable.** Deliver on the promises you make, and take ownership for your choices and decisions without blaming others or inventing alibis.
- **Be strong.** Exemplify an unmistakable commitment to facing reality, no matter how challenging that may be.

- The union steward who promises you the world if you join the union, but has a reputation for not keeping his word.
- A team leader who tells her employees to bring grievances through proper channels, but frequently flies off the handle and yells at her employees when issues arise.
- A peer coach who directs his mentee not to make assumptions, while he is making assumptions about what his mentee did, thought, or felt.

Clearly, you do not want to emulate the behavior in these examples. They represent the opposite of trustworthy role modeling. Your effectiveness in supporting others to take responsibility will be predicated on how responsible you are perceived to be. The box gives more details about how to inspire others through your example.

Now that you are in a good place and feel confident that someone can trust you, your primary task is to help the other person see her role in the situation. Remind her that while she may not have had control over what happened, she does have control over how she chooses to respond.

Once she agrees to take responsibility for her response, you may help her by asking her the questions listed in this chapter. Much of her work will be in her head and heart, and she may need time away from you to wrestle with accepting full responsibility and taking action. In many cases, you may need to pose the same question time and time again before she can own everything that is hers to own in the situation.

>> *Trust Tip*   *When people are feeling vulnerable and in pain, they tend to project their feelings onto others, particularly onto leadership. Helping people to accept responsibility for how they respond to betrayals supports both them as individuals and the organization as a whole.*

Taking responsibility is indeed very tough and personal work. You support the other person by acknowledging his courage, offering your own, and recognizing the actions that he is taking to rebuild trust and apply the lessons learned. Remember to celebrate every small step, for those small steps add up to significant movement forward toward renewal.

6

Forgive Yourself
and Others

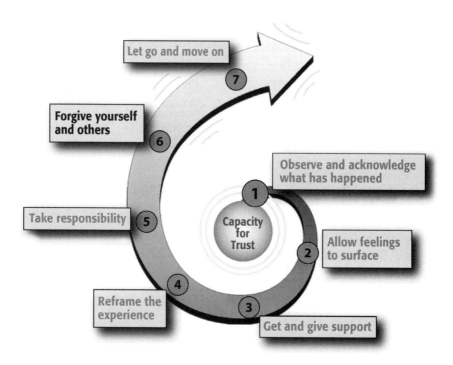

"To forgive is to set a prisoner free and discover that the prisoner was you."

—Lewis B. Smedes

Through reframing and taking responsibility, you have shifted from blame and judging to understanding—understanding about what happened and why, and understanding about your choices, opportunities, and lessons. You have embraced what is yours to own. Step Six, Forgiving Yourself and Others, is about using compassion as your partner to transition from that foundation of understanding and responsibility to the courage of letting go in Step Seven.

In forgiving, you ask what needs to be said or done to put this situation to rest. With forgiveness, you create your future by working through your feelings and changing your attitude about the past. Forgiveness allows you to heal from being hurt or let down, or from the pain of recognizing that you hurt someone else. When you don't forgive, you block your healing and thereby betray yourself. How? By not giving yourself the gift of growing from the experience. Importantly, forgiveness is not about forgetting. While you let go of blame and judgment, you continue to grasp the lessons you learned. Those lessons are often deep truths about yourself.

Authentic forgiveness of yourself and others is emancipating. In forgiving, you free yourself from the burden of bitterness and resentment. You let go of the need to judge others and yourself. Blaming and begrudging others depletes your energy and spirit, and interferes with your relationships and performance. Forgiveness frees blocked positive energy and dissipates destructive negative energy so that you can get back to work and life with renewed confidence and commitment.

To support your healing, consider and gain clarity on the answers to the following questions:

? What are the reasons why you are not able or willing to forgive?

What are signs or indicators that you have not forgiven?

How does not forgiving play out in your professional life?

How does not forgiving play out in your personal life?

Forgive Yourself

It may be obvious that you need to forgive yourself if you were the one to betray someone else. But if you were the one who was hurt, forgiveness of self may be less obvious. Many times, people who were betrayed look back at the situation and beat themselves up for having put themselves in the position to be hurt:

> *"How could I have been so naïve? How could I have been so foolish? If only I had asked more questions."*

No matter your role in the situation, you begin to forgive yourself by acknowledging that you did the best you could at the time. Perhaps, for whatever reason, it wasn't enough—but it was what it was. Beating yourself up mentally and emotionally is worthless and self-defeating. Re-spinning situations in your head is unproductive for you and for everyone around you. Such behavior depletes the energy you need in order to choose alternative, more productive courses of action and find compassion for the other person. Just as you cannot love another until you love yourself, you cannot forgive another until you forgive yourself.

Forgiving yourself is therefore more fundamental and as important as forgiving others. In forgiving yourself, be candid, clear, courageous, and responsible.

- **Be candid** in honestly facing the facts, admitting any wrongdoing and/or your faults, and acknowledging the pain you caused others or yourself.

- **Be clear** in your head by putting your inner critic on mute and letting go of any shame so that you can make way for an open, forgiving heart.

- **Be courageous** in facing your fears and other self-imposed barriers.

- **Be responsible** in identifying precisely what you are forgiving yourself for.

Above all, extend compassion to yourself. Pema Chödrön, Buddhist nun, author of *When Things Fall Apart* and resident teacher at

The Cost of Not Forgiving

There's a high cost of not forgiving: instead of freeing yourself from pain, you continue to carry emotional "baggage" around with you. When you don't forgive, you are likely to experience these symptoms:

- **Decreased energy and enthusiasm:**

  You are contaminated by bitter feelings, such as anger, resentment, and cynicism.

- **Decreased commitment and morale:**

  You feel deep resignation and have an "I don't care anymore" attitude.

- **Decreased confidence in self and others:**

  You become unwilling to take risks and collaborate with others.

- **Decreased openness and flexibility:**

  You become rigid in your thinking and acting, closed to new ideas, methods, and ways of solving problems.

- **Decreased health and well-being:**

  Your negative emotions may manifest themselves in your body as physical illness, anything from constant colds to cancer.

- **Decreased capacity to trust and be trusted by others:**

  If you don't forgive and trust yourself, you won't be able to forgive and trust others.

Gampo Abbey in Nova Scotia, encourages each of us to have compassion for the parts of us that we are not proud of, that "we feel are not worthy of existing on the planet."[1]

The parts that Chödrön speaks of refer to what is sometimes called our "shadow side." Dr. Carl Jung coined this term to describe the unconscious, undeveloped, and denied aspects of us that include the dark, rejected parts. Though we tend to be unaware of our shadow side, it significantly influences our behavior and often contributes to our role in a betrayal situation. Becoming more aware of our shadow side will help us to feel compassion, first for ourselves, and then for others. When we accept our shadow side, we are more able to forgive others and ourselves and move on.

Forgive Others

> *"The weak can never forgive. Forgiveness is the attribute of the strong."*
> —Mahatma Gandhi

While forgiving others is most necessary for those who have been hurt, this underlying process of extending compassion to others is important to everyone involved in the situation—whether you are the one hurt, the one who hurt another, or someone seeking to help others rebuild trust.

Forgiveness does not mean that you condone the betrayal behavior. In forgiving, you are not saying that the act of betrayal was okay. You are simply saying that you understand and that you have learned from the experience.

In the 2006 movie *Peaceful Warrior* based on Dan Millman's novel *The Way of the Peaceful Warrior*, the Dan Millman character says, "The hardest ones to love are usually the ones who need it the most."[2] This concept is also very true of forgiveness: The hardest ones to forgive are those who need it the most. The one who needs it most is the person who hurt you, and that's why you'll find more information about how to forgive others in the "When You Have Been Betrayed" section that follows.

> *"If you knew the secret history of those you would like to punish, you would find a sorrow and suffering enough to disarm all your hostility."*
>
> —Henry Wadsworth Longfellow

Over the last two decades of working with people at all levels in building and rebuilding trust in the workplace, we have experienced the incredible power of forgiveness in repairing broken working relationships. Forgiveness is strength and there is power in humility. When the forgiveness is genuine, there is power in the moment. The spirit of forgiveness moves people: old grudges are forgotten, festering wounds are healed and bad blood is cleansed and turned into thriving new partnerships. It takes courage and compassion to ask for forgiveness, and it takes greater courage and compassion to forgive yourself and others. Forgiveness will prob-

> *It takes courage and compassion to ask for forgiveness*

ably be the most challenging Step along your healing journey. You will need to muster up all of your energy, collect all your compassion, and do what you have been avoiding for a long time.

When You Have Been Betrayed

> *"I need to forgive myself for being so naïve. I was working hard and doing all I could to keep up, and I was blindsided. Now I know better. I will forgive the person for betraying me, because carrying the anger is wearing me down. But I will never forget the lessons I have learned— nor should I. They were too costly to gain and too valuable to forget."*

When someone betrays you, your feelings can range from mild frustration to significant disappointment and, in some cases, all the way to hate. In this emotional space, it is very natural and easy to focus on the other person and what they did. But in order to be able to forgive your betrayer, you need to shift that focus from that person to your wounded self.

First seek to forgive yourself for your role in the situation. Time and again, we hear people who have been betrayed say things like:

> *"I was ashamed that I had been duped. Aren't I smarter than that?"*

> *"Haven't I been around the block a time or two? Shouldn't I have seen this coming?"*

"Am I not smarter than this? How could I have let myself be put in this position?'

"Did I let pride get in the way of reason? Am I too arrogant to think I could be tricked?"

"Am I a professional failure because I got distracted by what was going on at home?"

"Am I weak because I was ill and therefore vulnerable? Will I be able to continue my career?"

"Why am I so sensitive? I wish I could just "toughen up" at work so things would roll off of me like they do for others."

Beating yourself up with questions like these does no good whatsoever. Make the distinction between the "look within yourself" aspect of reframing and unproductive self-bashing. Yes, you need to understand what was going on for you that allowed you to be hurt or caused you to react the way you did. Take that understanding, decide what you have to gain from addressing the underlying issue, and move on. When you accept who you are and take action to go forward, you forgive yourself. Reciting affirmations (see box) solidifies your commitment to self-forgiveness.

Forgive Others

Forgiving your betrayer begins by *detaching yourself* from that person. It takes significant inner strength and compassion to forgive, especially in the case of a major intentional betrayal. It takes courage to resist striking back and to take the high road. It takes courage to distance yourself from the instinct to seek revenge, as exemplified by this story Michelle shares about her late father.

During the Korean War, my father, Jack R. Chagnon, was held in captivity by the Chinese for almost forty months. The camp in which he was confined was located in Northern Korea along the Chinese border, a desolate part of the world with extraordinarily long, cold winters. The quality of life in the prison was deplorable, beyond what any of us can imagine. Dad recounted the forgiveness he extended upon his release to a prison mate we'll call "Sergeant," even though that man betrayed him and brought him considerable hardship.

At night we slept in grass huts on dirt floors. We were dying like flies. During the day we walked and walked and walked. We knew that if we stopped, we'd die. We lived from meal to meal. We would get one maggot-infested bowl of sorghum, soybeans, or millet in the morning around eight and the second one in the afternoon around four; that was it.

We were all weak and emaciated. I don't think I weighed 100 pounds. Hungry and cold all the time, we lived in constant fear that we'd get sick. It was an environment where everybody was fighting for survival. Some prisoners looked out for themselves at the expense of other people by ratting on them for candy, cigarettes, or extra bowls of rice.

When a fellow American prisoner, "Sergeant," ratted on me to the Chinese guards, I experienced an even more grueling phase of my captivity. It was all about socks. As prisoners, we wore thin canvas sneakers. One winter, it was so cold that our captors gave us each a threadbare blanket. I cut off a corner off my blanket and made myself a pair of socks with it. I could put my feet in these makeshift socks and then slip them into the sneakers. They would give me a little bit of protection from the extremely cold weather.

One day the Chinese shook down our barracks and found that I had cut my blanket. A buddy told me Sergeant had ratted on me for an extra bowl of rice.

I had to go before the camp commandant and two Chinese officers to explain my actions. I answered that my feet were cold and I was standing out in the snow all day with canvas sneakers. My punishment was three months alone in a hole in the ground in a constant state of bitter coldness. To this day, I do not know how I survived it.

Several months after my release, I was approached by my Company Commander who asked me if I knew of Sergeant's "collabora-

---

Affirmations

An affirmation is a positive statement in the present tense. Saying precise words frequently helps materialize what you are trying to create. In this case, you are trying to create forgiveness. The daily practice of making affirmations helps shift your energy from blaming another to having compassion for yourself or others.

Here are some general affirmations that support forgiveness:

"I forgive myself for having hurt others."

"I forgive others for having hurt me."

"I forgive myself for being in a personal place that let others hurt me."

Here are some affirmations to support forgiving yourself:

"I forgive myself for not delivering the project on time because I was dealing with personal problems in my family."

"I forgive myself for being naïve; because I know deep down that I want to trust others."

"I forgive myself for being distracted by illness, because I did the best I could with the energy and the stamina I had."

"I forgive myself for being so careless, rude, and insensitive to others because I was rushing to get the project done on time."

---

tion" with the Chinese while we were in captivity. I said yes, I know what he did. The Commander went on to ask if I would cooperate with formal Court Martial proceedings against him. I replied that I would, but only if I was ordered to do so; I didn't want to do anything to hurt him.

When I asked Dad how it was that he came to forgive Sergeant, he shared that when he was in captivity, his focus was on staying alive. When he was released, his focus was on living his life and building a future for himself. He said that he came to discover that during adversity some people lose hope and in that lost hope they betray others along with themselves. In time, he saw Sergeant as a desperate man who had lost hope and succumbed to disgraceful behavior. Dad also learned that it was not in his own makeup to lose hope in such a way.

> *And you know, I've gone through life with my head held high. I kept faith with myself. While I was in captivity, I did absolutely nothing to embarrass my country. I have always felt good about that. I like what I see when I shave in the mirror. And, there is not a person from that prison camp who I couldn't meet on the street and look right in the eye. I am proudest of the fact that I refused to cozy up to the Chinese.*

Forgiveness may be likened to a kind of "spiritual cleansing," a cleaning of the clutter of the wrongs your betrayer did to you and a separation of the person from the deed. You started this process as you reframed the situation by looking at your betrayer's experience and the circumstances that contributed to his behavior. In forgiveness, through the lens of compassion, you choose to look at your betrayer differently. You may see her as a person who is struggling with her own pain. Or, as in the case of Michelle's father, a person who had lost hope.

You may offer the benefit of the doubt. You may consider:

> ▣ Is it possible that she lost her sense of herself? Is it possible she betrayed herself in the process of betraying me?

> Was she in a tight position that caused her to feel threatened, frightened, or confused? Perhaps she was afraid she was going to lose something important to her?

To find compassion, consider that this person, in the moment, was doing the best he could do. When you do, you are able to see your betrayer as a person with needs, feelings, and vulnerabilities rather than an evildoer from the dark side. When it comes right down to it, we are all mirrors of each other. At the deepest level, we are like others and others are like us. Your betrayer just may have been stressed, up against a wall, and doing the best he could given his circumstances, and lost his footing, just as you have, many times.

Extending compassion to someone who has hurt you is challenging work. You rise to this challenge by stepping momentarily away from your own needs and pain in order to gain understanding of what might have contributed to the hurtful behavior.

One of our clients who works for a defense contractor laid out how he discovered the broader context for his betrayer's actions:

> *"My boss took my work and passed it off as his without giving me credit. At first, I could only see him as overly ambitious. But I wanted to heal, and I wasn't getting anywhere with that negative perspective. So I asked myself, 'is this characterization true? If so, why?'*
>
> *I determined that it is true . . . he is 'overly ambitious.' He is driven to be the President of our company. And, he is moving there as quickly as possible.*
>
> *The more powerful question was, 'Why? Is he a selfish, arrogant SOB or is it something else?' Well, while his ego is immense, I had seen too much evidence negating that it was blind, simple ego that drove this man. Then what was it?*
>
> *I have come to believe that he was driven by service to the nation and his drive to head the company came from his desire to set it on the greatest path to achieve this service mission. He is a patriot! And that is a position I can support."*

When you seek to understand, you express compassion and see the person in a different way. When you go to the next step and see yourself in his actions, you find not only compassion and forgiveness, but also self-awareness, healing, and possibility. You can then rebuild the relationship with the other person, and the relationship with yourself that was lost through the betrayal.

Recognize Forgiveness

How do you know when forgiveness has begun? Answer: When you can think about individuals who betrayed you and, with a sense of

Finding Compassion through Reflection

Begin to find compassion by asking yourself what might have been going on for the person who hurt you:

❓ What do you think might have caused this person who betrayed you to act in this way?

Is it possible he was in pain and lost his sense of himself?

Is it possible that she has betrayed herself in the process of betraying you?

You may find further compassion by reflecting on your own experiences of having betrayed another:

❓ Have you ever lost your own sense of self and behaved in ways that you were not proud of?

Have you ever behaved in a way that was not in keeping with your true nature?

Have you ever behaved in a way similar to the way that this person hurt you?

And finally, ask yourself what to do with your answers to the above questions:

❓ How can you communicate from the heart to un-stick a stuck situation?

How can you extend compassion to unfreeze an unworkable, frozen relationship so that some kind of understanding and considerate exchange begins to happen?

---

inner peace, wish them well. In situations where people are unwilling and unable to come together with you, you can still forgive them and free your mind and your heart. Reconciliation is not necessary for forgiveness to happen, or for your own healing to take place. You can still work through the process of the Seven Steps for Healing on your own to achieve the freedom and lightness you desire and the growth opportunity presented to you in the form of this challenge.

In many instances, full healing occurs when you invite the person back into your life. This part is challenging because it depends as much on the other person as on you. Both parties have to be willing to come together. You want your betrayer to listen to you and hear your claims, acknowledge and honestly apologize for what she did, understand the depth of the pain she caused you and feel the hurt you felt, and make new promises that she intends to keep.

Given that true reconciliation is a reciprocal process, she will want exactly the same from you. When both parties can make their expectations and commitments to each other clear, the relationship can heal and grow.

When You Have Betrayed Others

Hurting others can be unintentional and does not mean that you are a bad person. We all hurt others through unintentional oversights, rushing, and cramming to do more with less time, energy, and money. We tend to betray others when we override our own needs. The more self-aware you are, the more you feel the pain you cause others through such common and understandable behaviors, the more you can minimize your tendency to hurt others, and thereby yourself, in the future.

When you forgive yourself for betraying another, you decide to switch from beating yourself up (which does no good) to having compassion for yourself. You switch from blaming yourself to understanding yourself and the lessons that can help you at work and in life.

One way to "cut yourself some slack" is to make a distinction between your *behavior* that caused pain and yourself as a person. Behavior is momentary, your character is permanent; one is *what you did*, the other *who you are*. Nina, whose story of divulging a colleague's confidence we shared in Steps Two and Five, described her self-forgiveness as follows:

> *"I have forgiven myself because I now see that I was scared and vulnerable and feeling alone. In that place, I slipped. It doesn't mean I slipped as a person. It means I slipped in that moment in time."*

Another client said:

> *"I forgive myself because my moment of weakness does not make me a bad person. I made a mistake, I regret it, and I will work not to do it again."*

Yet another client, Tyler, carried the pain for years after graduation of having betrayed a business school classmate. As they had gone their separate ways, he had been unable to work to a place of healing with her. He had to find reconciliation within himself. He was finally able to stop mentally "beating himself up" when he realized that, yes, he made a mistake, and he learned some painful, but powerful lessons. He came to understand that, while he couldn't change the past, he could alter his behavior in the future. When he was able to have compassion for himself, he was able to forgive and be at peace with himself.

Recognize Self-Forgiveness

You know you are forgiving yourself when you:

- Can move from beating yourself up to finding lessons and moving on;
- Feel strong enough in your compassion to have a full reconciliation with the person you hurt;
- Can look in the mirror and feel good about yourself again;
- Have the sense of inner peace that comes from knowing that you did the best you could, given the circumstances; and
- Are able to deal with bigger trust challenges more effectively without beating yourself up so harshly or for so long.

When You Want to Help Others Rebuild Trust

"He that cannot forgive others breaks the bridge over which he, too, must pass."

—Lord Herbert
British philosopher and theologian

It is an honor and a privilege to help another in her healing process, and it is a powerful experience when someone allows you to support her in her journey. Because forgiveness is all about compassion, your support in this Step is all about the safe container you create to support the other person in order for her to let go of negative feelings, forgive, and move on. That container is made from the trust she has in you as you accompany her through this passage from pain to peace.

In many situations, especially those in which people perceive that trust is broken at an organizational level, employees cannot forgive leaders and the organization because they are still holding them and it accountable for the betrayal: They are still stuck in the blame mode. When dozens, hundreds, and even thousands of your colleagues are in that negative place, helping them to forgive is a huge task that will probably take more resources and time than you have at your disposal.

We recommend that you concentrate on helping individuals or a handful of people at a time; we call this process creating "pockets of readiness" with people who are willing to hear and embrace your message. Know that, as they heal, they will pass their renewed confidence, commitment, and energy on to others, maybe even by supporting other people in healing.

While it can seem next to impossible to move people who are in pain to forgiveness, you can make a difference simply by asking the right questions (see box above). In so doing, you help people shift from negative feelings to seeing positive possibilities. You can then go the next Step and work with them to find the solutions.

Helping People Shift from Blame to Forgiveness

Ask these questions to help someone forgive:

> **?** What do you need in order to resolve the issues, concerns, fears, and pain that you are feeling?
>
> What conversations need to take place?
>
> What still needs to be said? What needs to happen for healing to occur?
>
> What will make a difference right now?
>
> What does forgiveness look like to you?
>
> What is the impact of not forgiving?

Remember that healing and, in particular, forgiveness, take time, commitment, and plenty of patience. You may have to move very slowly, and you will definitely need compassion while you proceed. For most people, forgiveness happens one small step at a time. They have more layers of hurt feelings to unfold before they are totally willing to let go and move on. As one poetic client expressed it to us, "It is as though I am peeling the petals from the rose that forgiveness is—a beautiful, fragrant, unfolding process. Each petal of forgiveness is an invitation to a newer and richer level of understanding about others and myself."

For most people, forgiveness happens one small step at a time

Let Go
and Move On

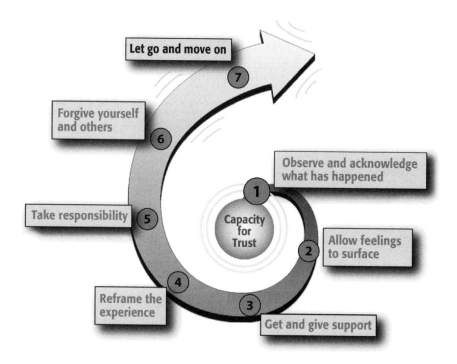

*"Whatever you can do, or dream you can, begin it.
Boldness has genius, power and magic in it."*

—Johann Wolfgang von Goethe

With courage and compassion, you have taken responsibility for the breach of trust through your actions or reactions (Step Five), and also forgiven yourself and others (Step Six). You have been moving through pain and guilt and are now ready to let go, in order to create an open space in the relationship in which trust can be rebuilt and renewal can happen.

Together, forgiveness, letting go, and moving on realign you with your sense of self. By being more fully aware of who you are, you expand your capacity for trust in yourself and others. The healing process is not about changing *who* you are; it is about becoming *more deeply aware* of who you are and honoring yourself.

Whether you were hurt or hurt someone else, in this Step you come to accept what has changed or been lost and what can't be changed or regained. Once you let go, you free your energy for moving forward in productive ways. You are ready to go on with life, stronger and more self-aware, self-accepting, and confident than before the trust was broken. In moving on, you choose to act differently as you look forward rather than backward. As Michelle's father did in Step Six, you focus on living life in the future rather than in the past.

Accept What Is So

In accepting what is so, you do not condone what was done to you or what you did, but you experience the reality of what happened without denying, disowning, or resenting it. In other words, you are able to let go of your ego and accept what happened without judgment and blame. You accept what can and cannot be changed without anger, guilt, remorse, or shame.

Without blame or guilt, you become aware of what you can and cannot control. In that way, letting go is a process of surrender. You give up the emotional baggage that clutters your mind and heart and interferes with your relationships. Letting go is like cleaning out your closet and actually throwing the junk away instead of just moving the stuff to another room in your house.

The Risk of Not Letting Go and Moving On

When you do not let go of your pain and move on from your hurt, you risk becoming a person who:

- **Does not trust herself**, thereby reducing self-confidence and commitment

  Charlotte seems to lack the self-assurance to stand up for herself in meetings and express her perspective, particularly when it may be viewed as unpopular.

- **Does not trust others,** thereby contributing to having difficulty with collaboration

  Rolf plays everything close to the chest and does not share important information that his co-workers need to do their job.

- **Acts erratically** at times, with behavior that is often problematic

  Geoff is a leader who rants and raves at team meetings when he is not getting his way.

- **Harbors ill feelings** toward others and is unforgiving of self and others

  Suzanne is still complaining about how she felt wronged by Mary over three years ago.

- **Sees only the "all" or "nothing"** in situations and people instead of being open to the gray area in between the extremes of "black and white"—the space that gives people permission to be human

  John tends to view people as right or wrong, good or bad. You mess up once with him and you're done for—end of story.

- **Jumps to negative conclusions and blame** prior to checking out assumptions

  Martha automatically assumes that people let her down. She never asks questions to see what's going on before leaping to conclusions.

In letting go, you are able to regain power that you may have given away when you were betrayed or when you betrayed another. In so doing, you are able to free up stuck emotional energy and mobilize it for making the necessary changes in your personal and professional life.

Letting go is in many ways the culmination of all of the other Steps you have gone through on your trust rebuilding journey, so if you are having trouble accepting what is so without blame or guilt, use these questions to help you figure out which Step you might need to repeat in order to resolve issues and complete unfinished work:

? What needs to be said or done to put this issue to rest?

Where is additional healing work needed?

Or, more specifically:

- Have you discovered a deeper layer of pain not directly related to this situation?

  ➤ Go back to Step Two to surface feelings associated with that situation, and then get support to work through them (Step Three).

- Do you worry that the same thing will just happen again?

  ➤ Go back to Step Three and get support to help you reframe (Step Four) and look at the positive possibilities.

- Do you still find no reason or rationale for the way you or the other person acted?

  ➤ Go back to Step Four to look deeper into the other person's experience and within yourself to find a context that can help you to understand why the situation may have occurred.

- Are you still feeling that you have no power in this situation?

  ➤ Go back to Step Five, Take Responsibility, to see what part you own and discover actions you can take.

- Are you still beating yourself up for your actions or reactions?

  ➤ Go back to Step Six to work on forgiving yourself and others.

How You Know When You Are Ready to Move On

"Gratitude is the sign of noble souls."

—Aesop

Through compassion for yourself and others, you have come to see everyone's point of view and become able to forgive. Forgiveness has opened the door to inner peace. You know that you are ready to move on when you are able to reflect on the experience and feel that sense of inner peace. When you have let the learning sink in, you feel solace wash over you. You no longer feel anxiety, anger, or tension when the other person comes into the room or if his name is mentioned in conversation. You have let go of slipping into self-pity for what was "done to you" by the other person, and have taken full responsibility for your part in the unfolding dynamics. You now know that you have let go and are ready to move on. Things will seem to fall into place in a synchronous way when you surrender and allow the healing process to take its due course.

When you have let the learning sink in, you feel solace wash over you.

Another sign that you have let go and are ready to move on is that you are grateful for having gone through the experiences, as painful as they were, and have a sense of appreciation regarding the relationship and lessons learned. Not easy tasks, we know. That's why, in the quote opening this section, Aesop invoked the term "noble souls."

Here's what one of our clients, Gus, told us nine months after the trust rebuilding process in his department:

"It is time to let go and move on. I've learned some lessons—difficult as they were. I have spent enough time, energy, and emotion on this experience for a lifetime. I would not want to go through this again, but I am grateful for the experience and the lessons it provided me. It has strengthened me, and I'm glad it's over!"

If you have truly let go, you have feelings of gratitude for the other people involved, whether they hurt you or reacted to your

Knowing You Have Healed

How, then, do you know you have come to the end of this healing journey? When:

- You are able to let go of your ego and accept what has happened without judgment and blame.
- You are able to reflect on the experience of betrayal and have a sense of gratitude and inner peace. Yes, there may still be a dull pang of pain, but your tears no longer flow.
- In looking back over the experience of betrayal, you reflect what you learned about others and yourself and find wisdom that you will use in the future.
- You identify what you will do differently next time. You gain clarity about your approach to future relationships.
- You don't forget what happened. You remember so that you take other and future relationships to new heights of connection and trust.

actions. You can experience that gratitude, whether or not you were able to fully mend the relationship. Being grateful for those who challenge you is a task much easier said than done, for you often resent those people and their behavior in the moment, or are frustrated and angry with them for causing you pain.

> *"If you want to turn your life around, try thankfulness. It will change your life mightily."*
>
> —Gerald Good

Gratitude can also be a catalyst to help you reframe and transform the experience. You may therefore find yourself repeating Step Four at a deeper level. Giving thanks for the lessons learned and the benefits gained helps you change your attitude from loss to gain. You

---

» Trust Tip   *We know we are ready to move on when we are able to reflect on the experience and have a sense of gratitude for the lessons gained.*

appreciate the growth this life experience has given you. Being appreciative of the lessons learned, versus bemoaning the loss and cost, helps to shift your attitude and your life from negative to positive.

Moving On Is Choosing to Act Differently

"You may never know what result comes of your action, but if you do nothing there will be no result."

—Mahatma Gandhi

Unburdened by judgment and blame, you are free to act differently. You allow possibilities to come into your life that were not options while you were bogged down and stuck in past pain. You allow yourself to renew relationships with yourself and others.

Learning to relate to yourself or others in a different way, with heightened awareness, takes practice, time, patience, and self-care.

Like learning a new skill, learning to relate to yourself or others in a different way, with heightened awareness, takes practice, time, patience, and self-care. Start with small steps. Experiment with what works and what doesn't. You are like the farmer going through all the necessary steps in order to be able to reap a fine harvest in the fall: you have prepared the soil, sowed the seeds, watered and weeded, fought off pests, and made careful decisions about pruning—all so that you are able to harvest the rewards months later.

In healing broken trust, your reward is moving on, not only with the relationship in question, but also with the rest of your life.

Take Gus, for example, whom we quoted earlier in the discussion about gratitude. His entire team chose to act differently after the trust rebuilding process. Lines of communication opened up between leadership and employees, and greater collaboration took place between people and departments in accomplishing goals. Gus also learned lessons that changed his personal behavior. When he had an issue with colleagues, he took it directly to them, rather than complaining about them to everyone else. He became brutally honest in admitting his mis-

---

Reaching New Heights

When you have let go, you are free to act differently. It's as if you have a blank canvas to fill. What does that mean in practice? You have:

- **Heightened awareness:** You may notice that you are experiencing new sensations, thoughts, and feelings.

  When in an argument with a co-worker over a job-related problem, I no longer need to make the other person wrong in order for me to be right.

- **A fresh outlook:** You may see old things in a new way.

  When I am asked to change how I work, I now am more open to looking at how to make that adaptation rather than justifying why it can't be done.

- **A more open mind:** You may gain greater clarity regarding how to resolve problems with co-workers.

  When I am confronted with a conflict situation at work, I now check out the facts rather than make assumptions.

- **Greater flexibility:** You may have freed blocked energy that causes rigidity. You now have greater flexibility of mind and spirit.

  I have let go of my territorial posture and I am more willing to collaborate with others.

---

takes and taking responsibility to correct them. That approach fostered a sense of safety for others to admit and own *their* errors. He was impeccable in keeping his agreements and supporting his co-workers in meeting their deliverables. His department results increased an unprecedented 25 percent—the highest single increase in the company's history. His boss was elated, and Gus felt relieved and vindicated.

Reflection Questions

Describe a situation in which you let go and moved on.

What did you do? What did letting go and moving on look like for you?

What gain did you make? What was the impact on others?

Integrate and Celebrate

When you took action in Step Five, you began to change the way you behave. At that point, you may only have been acting differently toward that one person or in similar situations. Now, as you move on, you transfer that learning to other aspects of your life. It may be that in healing from a workplace betrayal, you develop new ways of acting or reacting that you can carry into your personal relationships.

As you let go and move on, you come to know that all that has happened was for a higher purpose. Sometimes that higher purpose stretches far beyond the situation at hand. In letting go, you sometimes move on to another deeper layer of hurt and betrayal that may take you from the workplace into your personal life, or maybe even back to betrayals you experienced in childhood. Letting go of this one betrayal may then be a gateway into much deeper learning and growth.

At this point, you know you can't slide back into old habits. You know too much about trust, relationships, the other person involved, and, most importantly, *yourself.* You hold yourself to a higher level of integrity and responsibility.

The same client who gave us the image of forgiveness as a rose (Step Six) expressed the power of healing in this way:

> *"Healing from betrayal is analogous to scar tissue after a wound: the scar is often more robust and tough than the original tissue. And so it may be for human interactions."*

Above all, in Step Seven it is important to celebrate how far you have come. If you have experienced either side of a minor betrayal, your celebration may simply be noting your growth to yourself. You may go a step further to write what you've learned in your journal.

Marisol, whom we met in Step Two as she took time off after feeling betrayed from learning in a performance review about teammates' complaints, celebrated the culmination of her year long healing journey by taking an extended vacation.

Celebrate Success

Use these questions to help identify growth to celebrate:

? What do you notice about yourself?

Where are there early successes to acknowledge and celebrate?

What do you feel good or proud about?

What would you like to acknowledge yourself for?

What gift would you like to give to yourself to celebrate your healing and growth?

Pierre, a manufacturing plant supervisor who was demoted to an assembly line worker during a company merger, went on a trout-fishing expedition to a remote lake high in the mountains to be by himself and appreciate his newfound freedom as a line worker with decreased job-related stress.

When You Have Been Betrayed

In this section, we are going to follow the story of Stephen as he comes to accept what is so, integrates the gains he made from healing, and moves on in a way that drives not only his life, but also that of others, in exciting new directions. As this introduction to Stephen's story shows, he acknowledged what happened (Step One) and allowed his feelings to surface (Step Two).

> Stephen was as good as they get in his field. As a sharp, young brand manager, he was aggressive and smart; he knew what he wanted and he went after it. For seven and a half years, he gave his heart and soul to his company. He was promoted and enjoyed a close working relationship with his boss. When the financial crisis hit, his company announced lay-offs, but Stephen felt safe. And he was, until he made an off-hand comment that his boss interpreted as an indication that he would lie to customers. "He didn't ask me to explain myself, did not give me the

benefit of the doubt, and did not stand up for me to his boss," Stephen recalls. Shortly thereafter, he was laid off.

Feeling angry, hurt, and ashamed that he lost his job, Stephen blamed himself. "I painfully relived that eventful conversation with my boss a thousand times, reviewing what I said and what I could have done differently." Filled with doubt, Stephen's mind was plagued with thoughts of "I am not good enough, I am not enough."

Although Stephen initially turned to drugs and alcohol to dull his pain, he ultimately accepted support, reframed the situation, took responsibility for his part and his reaction, and forgave himself and his boss. We'll pick up his story as he lets go and moves on.

Accept What Is So

Ultimately, in the stillness of the woods on a personal retreat, Stephen let go of the delusion of trying to kid himself by using drugs and alcohol. He got in touch with his priorities, how he wanted to be in his personal and professional relationships, and how he wanted to live his life. "I made the commitment to myself to clean up my act and find a job within eight weeks."

You do not have to go through a cycle of depression, drugs, and alcohol as Stephen did to be able to let go and move on. Like many of us when we are facing external challenging situations, Stephen's internal demons came to the surface. In his case, those demons were feelings of inadequacy and abandonment. In order to get at his core truth, he had to accept his shadow side (see Step Six) without judgment and blame.

Stephen came to be able to look back at his situation in his former job without judgment and blame and accept what was so.

Knowing You Are Ready to Move On

Within seven weeks of that retreat, Stephen landed a new job as the head of a division for a large company.

About a year after he was laid off, as he was sipping his morning coffee on an early spring day, Stephen realized that he was ready to move on. He felt grateful for having had such an abundance of support. "In the past, I had thought that asking for support was a sign of weakness, of incompetence. Now, I see it not only as the right thing to do, but the smart thing to do as a responsible adult."

He also took stock of how much he had learned. Stephen had come to realize that being a good husband and father was much more important to him than the amount of his paycheck. "Husband and father" more accurately defined him than "star employee." He had come to recognize that there is more to life than materialistic goods.

As he sat there that March morning, Stephen felt a wave of emotion come over him. It was part peace: He felt at ease with himself and he noticed that the tension he had carried in his neck began to lift. And it was also part excitement: A thread of electric energy pulsed through him as he thought about the opportunities that lay before him and heard his daughter call, "Daddy, pancakes are ready!"

When he freed himself of his emotional baggage, Stephen was able to calm his inner storm and find stillness. It was in this space of serenity that he let go and found self-acceptance. He got in touch with who he was and what was most important to him. It was in this quiet space that became ready to act differently.

Moving On is Choosing to Act Differently

Doing what he loved, Stephen quickly made a positive impact on the culture and the bottom line of his new company. He now has a different approach in how he views himself and how he treats others. We asked him how he had changed. Here's how he answered:

"I notice that I am more humble and more respectful of other people, particularly those who report to me. In the past, I had a 'rugged individual' attitude in order to get ahead. Now, I respect each employee's input and go to great lengths to include others, particularly in decisions that affect their jobs and their lives. Before, I would approach employees with a 'follow me as I carry the flag up the hill' attitude. Now, I follow them as they carry the flag up the hill.

I have also discovered the law of reciprocity: what I put out comes back to me tenfold. In my new role, I counsel others. I give value to them and I receive much more value in return."

Integrate and Celebrate

As a leader in his new company, Stephen is much more focused on taking care of and supporting his people to do their jobs rather than just bringing in results. He is developing an organizational culture of trust where leaders lead by example, and "live the work" by confronting reality. It is a work environment where issues are surfaced when they arise and are dealt with openly. Employees' input and opinions count. And if someone takes a responsible risk and it doesn't work out or even fails, she knows her supervisor will support her.

In addition, Stephen has made a strong commitment to developing the professional and technical skills of his employees. That commitment is beginning to pay off. Summarizes Stephen, "I see myself as a producer, as a developer of people and performance."

Within the first few months with his new company, Stephen had even taught his new boss a few lessons about developing leadership effectiveness and trustworthiness, such as being impeccable about keeping his word and delivering on promises to his employees. Asked what has helped him the most to succeed, Stephen responded, "By realizing that trust begins with me. That I can't expect my employees to do something and go somewhere that I am not willing to do or go first." As a result, Stephen has earned his employees' confidence, commitment, and endless energy.

When You Have Betrayed Others

The key aspect of letting go and moving on for those who have hurt others is choosing to act differently and integrating that change into your life in a broader context. Let's take a look back at a client we have brought up several times, Nina. In retrospect, Nina sees that the mistake she made by divulging Ted's confidence was "a defining point in [her] development as a leader." Here's how she expresses her growth:

"After I was able to forgive myself, I let go and moved on. Yes, it was a painful experience. It always hurts to look back and see that you lost yourself. But I am very grateful for the experience, because it contributed to who I am today."

Tyler, whose story of betraying a colleague in graduate school we told in Step Six, had reactions similar to Nina's:

"I learned a potent, painful lesson from that event: that we choose our behavior and there are consequences to that behavior. It took me some time to forgive myself. But I now do not feel bad about it. I recognize it for what it was.

Help Others Let Go and Move On

Here are some tips about effective ways to acknowledge others' positive movement in letting go and moving on:

- **Reinforce positive behavior.** Give positive feedback, and acknowledge the progress people are making. Doing so helps them to repeat and reinforce that behavior.

  "I noticed in our weekly meeting, Will, that you were asking a lot of good questions that help you to understand the issues that others are struggling with. I acknowledge you for seeking to understand before acting on assumptions or jumping to conclusions."

- **Be specific.** Acknowledge the specific behavior that you noticed and when you noticed it.

  "Patrick, I have noticed that, for the last two months, you have consistently been showing up five minutes early to our staff meetings. That reminded me of a conversation we had four months ago when you heard how your tardiness was impacting others; you said you wanted to change your behavior. I want to recognize you for following through. Congratulations!"

- **Be timely.** Because of the demands on our time, we often forget to give others positive feedback. Do so as soon as you can so that you don't forget and so that the specific situation is fresh in everyone's mind.

Years later I have been able to turn that episode of my life into something good. In my courses that I teach on conflict resolution at the university, I use myself and my behavior back then as an example to help others learn powerful lessons about trust in relationships."

When You Want to Help Others Rebuild Trust

When you want to help others let go and move on from broken trust in this advanced Step, your main role is to acknowledge the behavior changes that you see. You do so by giving people positive feedback for the new ways they are acting. Your feedback reinforces the new

"Alice, I noticed that you helped your new supervisor troubleshoot a computer problem this morning. It's fantastic that you are willing to help her "learn the ropes," particularly since you were originally a candidate for her job."

■ **Appreciate the benefit.** As people do their own work and rebuild trust in their lives, they are more present, open, and able to be in effective relationship with others and with themselves. Recognize this growth when you see people becoming able to help others at work and at home.

"Josephine, I want you to know that I recognize that you have changed your behavior for the better. Since you have stopped talking about others in the office, I have noticed that people on the team seem more willing to work with you. In fact, the whole team seems to be in a more trusting and productive place than it was a year ago."

■ **Celebrate the success.** Acknowledge and appreciate the lessons learned from mistakes, painful challenges, and even breaches of trust.

"Boy, Matt, I know you really had a tough week when a couple of folks you were relying on dropped the ball. But you worked through it with them and seemed to learn a few good lessons along the way. How about we go down to the pub and celebrate with a beer?"

behavior. The Box gives you key points to remember in acknowledging others' movement in the right direction.

By helping others to acknowledge the challenging road they have traveled and the progress they have made, you help them learn to rebuild trust and renew their confidence, commitment, and energy. It can be exceptionally uplifting to be present with someone when they realize how far they have come. We encourage you to take part in their celebration, for without you their journey would have been much harder. When you celebrate healing, you celebrate their discovery, their growth, their deepening sense of self, and the gifts they are now able to bring to others in their relationships.

Renewing Confidence, Commitment, and Energy

What we love most about our jobs is witnessing the moment when a person breaks through his or her pain to discover the release that comes with rebuilding trust and healing. We see the weight come off her shoulders, the stress dissipate from his face, and the gait in her step become more lively, assured, and purposeful.

When you rebuild trust in your relationships, you renew confidence in yourself and others, you restore a sense of commitment to your relationships and your workplace, and you regain your energy to deliver on your promises.

The Healing Journey

You grow when you choose to step into and work through your pain. You learn from your challenges and make difficulties work for you versus against you. Two of our clients, Peter and his boss, Daniel, experienced such powerful, meaningful growth in their relationships with each other, themselves, and their department. When we first met them, Peter was deeply disappointed that the collaborative work environment he was "sold" as a candidate turned out to feel disjointed, lonely, and accusatory.

Peter had uprooted his family to join this organization. He believed in its purpose and saw in his new boss, Daniel, a mentor. He was touched when Daniel indicated that he would have him to his home for dinner and help him become acclimated during the transitional period while Peter waited for his family to join him.

However, neither the mentoring nor the dinner invitations ever came to fruition. At first, Peter chalked it up to Daniel being busy. But when, over the course of his first year on the job, the focus was on short-term objectives rather than strategy, as promised in the interviews, Peter became more deeply disappointed. He did not experience mentoring from Daniel, who now seemed aloof, distant, and reactionary. While his relationship with Daniel was not what Peter wanted it to be, he continued to hope that that he could build a career at the organization.

Then, out of the blue, his world changed. Two team members accused Peter of making sexual comments in their presence. Without discussion, Daniel told Peter that he had no choice but to follow standard protocol and that HR would be launching a formal sexual harassment investigation. Daniel instructed Peter to go home immediately and make no contact with anyone until the investigation was completed. He gave the rest of the department only a very brief announcement that Peter was on leave immediately and indefinitely.

Peter remained at home, out of contact for six weeks. He could not imagine what led to the accusations. Periodically, he would hear from HR, but not from Daniel. Peter felt shut out, deeply confused, and disoriented.

Although the charge ended up being false and Peter resumed his responsibilities, the damage to his already disappointing relationship with Daniel seemed permanent. Realizing that the situation was untenable, they both summoned the conviction to work through the Seven Steps. Their journey brought them to a place of connection, closeness, and performance neither of them had imagined possible.

Step 1: Observe and Acknowledge What Happened

It wasn't until Peter discovered our book about trust building that he saw possibilities for improvement in his relationship with Daniel. Peter was able to put a word onto what he had long been feeling: betrayed. He gained perspective about what can be done to rebuild trust. Through the book, Peter observed and acknowledged on multiple levels what had happened in his relationship with Daniel.

With his family settled and his belief in the organization's mission still intact, Peter felt inspired to rebuild his relationship with Daniel. Peter invited Daniel into the exploration by giving him his copy and saying, "You need to read this book."

Through the book, Daniel realized that his relationship with Peter had been seriously damaged and that he had a role in that damage. He knew he had work to do and realized that he could not do it alone; he needed support.

In one-on-one work with Michelle and through the interview and survey data that she presented, Daniel was able to observe how he had let Peter down. He saw the impact on the entire department that came from not giving them more information about why Peter had been on leave. He was able to see that he had been blind as to how Peter's absence had impacted them; he had simply expected them to continue on as if nothing had happened.

Through one-on-one and department discussions, he then acknowledged how the situation had made them feel. He let them know that he understood that they had felt disoriented, confused, and angry about how the investigation had been handled. "I understand that I left you all hanging at a time when you needed more information," said Daniel in these meetings. "I understand why you would think I don't care. I acknowledge that it was inappropriate for me to expect you to continue on as if nothing ever happened. I see now that you experienced Peter's physical absence and my emotional distance as a double loss: You were confused and had no place to turn."

"When I finally sat down with Peter, I came to understand why he was so hurt. I had abandoned him during the investigation. I told Peter that while I did have to follow protocol, I certainly could have called to check in on him." Daniel acknowledged that he had not extended compassion to Peter and that he understood how alone he must have felt.

"I can now also understand the series of disappointments that preceded the charges," summarized Daniel. "I hear that he saw me as a potential mentor and I sure have not been that. He had me on a pedestal and I ended up disappointing him in so many ways. I was so completely unaware of his desires and the depth of pain I had caused him. I had said I would invite him to dinner—I barely remember that—but I never followed through."

Peter and Daniel observed what had happened in their relationship. Peter acknowledged the loss of relationship with Daniel and the impact that had on him: He had lost his dream of having a mentor; he had lost his vision of a trusting workplace where people treated each other with care. Daniel acknowledged that he was clueless regarding Peter's work-related expectations and desires. Daniel also acknowledged that he wasn't doing his job as a mentor, or as a leader to members of his team. He came to terms with the impact of his failure to pay attention.

Step 2: Allow Feelings to Surface

Because Peter had felt disappointed for a long time, and carried the pain of being wrongly accused, his feelings regarding his relationship with Daniel surfaced earlier than did Daniel's. "As I read the book, I found validation of what I had been thinking and feeling," recalls Peter. "It was as if someone opened my heart, looked into my soul, and saw my pain. My eyes began to well with tears as I realized I was not crazy and not alone."

For his part, Daniel didn't know about how he had hurt Peter until much later, when he was working with Michelle. "I was floored and flabbergasted when I heard how let down my team felt. Realizing the damage I had done to Peter was especially emotionally hard for me. I pride myself in not wanting to hurt anyone, yet I really had hurt him and those around him."

Peter and Daniel surfaced their feelings in different ways. When Peter read the book, he had a release that was liberating. He finally felt confirmation of thoughts and validation of feelings that had been rumbling around in his head and churning in his heart. When Daniel realized what he had done, he was caught off guard. He stopped to reflect upon his relationship with Peter. Realizing that his behavior had hurt Peter so much saddened Daniel. He struggled to express his feelings. He acknowledged that expressing his feelings in other aspects of his life was difficult as well, so this was all new learning for him.

Step 3: Get and Give Support

Daniel had listened to Peter regarding the need for support. "We brought in an outside coach to help us address the issues. Michelle helped open my eyes to the extent of the damage I had done. Her presence made it safe for me to talk through things with him."

Michelle also supported Peter to understand the layers of hurt he felt. She helped him move from his pain to reframing and taking responsibility for his part of what happened.

Likewise, Michelle supported the entire department by providing them with a venue to share their perspective and feelings about the way Peter's investigation and absence had been handled. The department relied on her to facilitate meetings so that they could continue to work through the Steps together.

With Michelle as a coach, Daniel, Peter, and the other members of the department were supported to rebuild trust in their relationships. Peter was able to shift from feeling like a victim and realize that both he and Daniel had choices regarding how they could interact with one another and how they could rebuild their relationship in a mutually beneficial way. Daniel used the support to learn about himself and find new ways of connecting with his team.

Step 4: Reframe the Experience

Reframing brought about a definite shift in both men. Daniel changed the way he interacts with his employees. Peter developed a willingness to open up to Daniel. Peter's shift came about when he started to see his boss differently.

"What made the relationship with Daniel change was his being willing to sit down and listen to me about the false sexual harassment charge and the series of letdowns that came before it. I told him, 'At a time when I needed you to back me, you pulled away and played it safe.' "

As he learned more about Daniel's resistance to express himself, Peter was finally able to reframe the situation and understand why Daniel had been unable to support him at that time. "It wasn't that he didn't care. It was simply that he didn't have the skills to be there for me."

For his part, Daniel reframed the experience by seeing Peter in a different way. "Through this process, I came to understand Peter's background," summarized Daniel. "He had had a tough childhood and had followed a winding path to success. I had thought of him as strong and confident since he had a brash, in-your-face tone. He was an extrovert who seemed to have it all worked out. Now I see that underneath that tough exterior, he had really deep needs for connection with a mentor and was looking for me to fill them. I'm the opposite: I'm an introvert who needs to be alone to think things through. I realize now that my tendency to avoid confrontation and emotion is what led to so much of the sense of abandonment that Peter and other members of my team experienced."

Peter and Daniel were able to look at how the extenuating circumstances and each other's behavioral preferences contributed to each of them reacting in ways that ultimately caused their relationship to break down. Once they were able to understand each other's experience (Peter feeling abandoned and Daniel retreating from confrontation and feelings), they were each able to look within themselves and understand that they had choices as to how to respond: They could continue to judge and blame the other, or they could seek to understand through compassion. From the lessons they learned, they also saw how they could rebuild their relationship and help the department to heal and grow.

Step 5: Take Responsibility

Even as the one who initially felt hurt, Peter sees that he had a role in what happened. "Looking back over my earlier interactions with Daniel, I now see that I read too much into what I heard during the interview process. I hoped for more than was offered. I needed to take responsibility for my part in working through the tough issues in order to give the relationship a second chance."

Daniel took responsibility for his behavior; specifically, for the way he treated people. Peter witnessed the result: "Daniel made more of an effort to be there for people. He is far less dismissive now. He really worked hard at making that change."

Daniel also took responsibility for avoiding conflict and for his behavior with the team. "Before we went through this trust rebuilding work, I never knew how others saw me. Now I see that my need to avoid confrontation meant that I had abdicated responsibility for leading my team. I now see that I didn't consider Peter's feelings when he was accused of sexual harassment because I didn't want to be involved in the conflict. I realize that people need connection with me. I am proud to be Peter's mentor."

Peter and Daniel each took responsibility for their part of the relationship breaking down. Peter realized that keeping thoughts and feelings to himself for all that time had been unfair to Daniel; they only grew in him and caused him to lose perspective. Peter also realized why Daniel hadn't been more present to him during the sexual harassment case. Daniel took ownership by understanding that his need to avoid confrontation meant that he had abdicated his responsibility to provide appropriate support to Peter. He also owned that his dismissive behavior hurt his effectiveness as a leader. Both men took action to correct their behavior and be there for the other. As a result, they started to realize what they had gained from this experience.

Step 6: Forgive Yourself and Others

Daniel remembers the forgiveness phase of their healing. "I first had to forgive myself. Yes, I had a responsibility to turn to HR and follow protocol. But I did not need to abandon Peter and my people. We both said we were sorry. Peter was able to express his needs clearly to me, and I agreed to support Peter by giving him developmental attention. I took action to address some lingering issues in the department, made some long overdue personnel changes, and promoted Peter to Assistant Vice President."

Peter and Daniel each apologized and made meaningful restitution to the other. Daniel also apologized to his people for not paying attention to the impact of the situation on them and for expecting them to go on as if nothing had happened. In addition, Daniel forgave himself. He moved from admonishing himself for his avoidance behavior to feeling compassion for himself. He acknowledged that he did the best he knew how to do at the time. Peter showed compassion for Daniel by shifting his anger to forgiveness. He also showed renewed commitment to Daniel and the company by "getting back in the game" and becoming a top performer once again.

Step 7: Let Go and Move On

After working with Michelle for three months, both Daniel and Peter were able to reflect upon the gains they had made.

"What makes the difference now is knowing that Daniel is going to listen to me, and not dismiss me—knowing that he is ready to hear me, and knowing there isn't going to be any judgment. The fact that he is willing to sit down and listen gives me the strength to talk about issues and be upfront with him about them. After all, in order to get through it, you've got to go through it."

Daniel said, "I think the act that shows I've let go and moved on is that I promoted Peter precisely because I have such confidence in him. I want to invest in his career. I have discovered that I actually enjoy mentoring."

Both Peter and Daniel have accepted what happened in their relationship without guilt or judgment. Each has integrated his learning into acting differently in support of their relationship. They now celebrate how far they have come and how much they appreciate one another. Sure, they have missteps. But when they occur, each takes responsibility for sustaining trust in their relationship.

The Outcome: Confidence, Commitment, and Energy

> *"Getting here was harder and took more effort than I ever thought. But, I and we would not be where we are today if we had not gone through it."*
>
> —Daniel

When you feel betrayed, you lose the confidence, commitment, and energy that keeps relationships together, fuels your performance, and feed your satisfaction at work. Now, through rebuilding trust with courage and compassion, you have healed and the restored those critical aspects of yourself. Peter and Daniel experienced these outcomes and articulated their gains in interviews with us a year after we worked with them.

The Healing Express

While Peter and Daniel took several months to move through the Seven Steps for Healing, many of the breaches of trust you'll experience may not require such a long journey. Take this example about how Lisa moved through a relatively minor situation in one afternoon.

> Lisa had been promoted to manage a team of seven. The team had previously been missing deadlines, making excessive mistakes, and failing to be responsive to internal customers. Her boss, Jared, asked her to turn things around and to hold people accountable. Lisa rose to the occasion and began to deliver results.
>
> Jared prepared to expand Lisa's responsibility in a way that would require tight collaboration with another team leader, Thomas. Jared met with Thomas to share his plans to expand Lisa's role and to review how Thomas would be involved in supporting Lisa in the transition. Jared was floored when Thomas responded by saying that he had heard several complaints about her from her team. Based on what he heard, Thomas did not think that Lisa was right for the job and therefore did not want to work with her.
>
> Jared brought Thomas and Lisa together to talk things through. He supported Thomas in putting his concerns on the table. Lisa felt blindsided. She had no idea that her people had been

Confidence

"I have learned that it's OK for us to be vulnerable as people, and that it's better to show your vulnerability rather than to hide it because the outcome will be better for everyone. When we're vulnerable, showing who we are, opening up, expressing our needs, we are true to ourselves. We trust in who we are and become confident in what we do."

—Peter

"Before going through this process, I tried pretending to be somebody I was not. Now I want to be real for my people. I am so much more willing to 'face the music' and take on the tough issues."

badmouthing her. She was further hurt that Thomas had not come to her with the issues he had been hearing. "We've known each other for a long time. I thought that by now you would know that I am willing to hear anything you need to bring to my attention."

Thomas heard her and took responsibility for playing a role in the grapevine by believing what he heard without checking it out. He told her what he had heard and listened to her perspective. He apologized for the potential damage to her and promised to never participate in the rumor mill again.

With Thomas's support, Lisa identified what she needed to address. She and Thomas, with Jared's support, talked through their collaboration plan. They agreed on how they would build trust in their relationship and between their respective teams. First and foremost, they promised to bring issues to one another's attention and to support one another to address them.

As they let go and moved on, they carried with them insight about how gossip can damage trust in relationships. They made a commitment not to participate in the grapevine and to redirect conversations when they saw the rumor mill in action. They were not willing to allow such behavior, while pervasive, to erode trust in their or their team's relationships.

"I used to be hesitant and unsure of myself when I talked to others. I know people thought I was aloof or abrupt. I was really just confused about who I was as a leader. Now, I know what it means to sit down and listen. I can connect much more easily with people these days. I enjoy the relationships that have emerged.

"I get this feeling that my heart has started opening up. The only person who was looking for me to be perfect was me. I feel much more comfortable to be a person around my direct reports. I can admit that I make mistakes, I can admit when I'm hurt or disappointed, and I can even put words on those feelings for the first time in my life. Before, I couldn't even talk about my emotions with my wife.

"All in all, I guess I finally understand what it means to be 'wholly present' with people. And underneath that, I am accepting who I am—not just as a leader, but also as a person."

—Daniel

When you rebuild trust, you start by rebuilding self-trust. In so doing, you regain confidence in yourself because you come to accept more fully who you are. In that way, you may, like Daniel, end up more confident to be yourself than you were before trust was broken. Being self-confident means that you are willing to bring "all of yourself" to the table, even the parts you fear that others may not like, because you believe that all in all, you are indeed "good enough." You, like Daniel, see yourself as competent and are willing to take personal risks.

This inner layer of healing allows you to restore your confidence in the other person or people involved, and in those you may have labeled "guilty by association." From there, you restore your confidence in the leadership of your organization or even in the innate goodness of humankind.

Commitment

"My relationship with Daniel now far exceeds anything I ever hoped for or thought possible. It is stronger than ever! I have moved from a time when I felt deceived, to now having even more than I ever hoped for in my working relationship with Daniel. I know that he'll have my back and I will have his!

"Daniel lets me be vulnerable. I am tremendously committed to him and to our company. He challenges me and holds me accountable. In return, he knows where my commitment and my loyalty lie. As a result of the trust building work we've done, I am able to perform at a very high level. My dedication to the company is also deeper than before.

"If I were to summarize the outcome of rebuilding trust across our department, I'd say that the company gets committed, performing employees who will go to the wall for the boss and the team. The greatest value I now experience is that I know people will do what they say they will do. And, if for some reason, they do not, we work it through. Things do not pile up. We used to be 'every man for himself.' Now, people care about one another. It is amazing what can happen when you know that people care about you."

—Peter

"I admit that I started this process because of the situation with Peter. But it's helped my relationship with all of my direct reports—and my colleagues at my level, too. Now that I know what's possible, I want to have the same kind of connection with everyone. And I sense that I do. What's even more exciting for me is to see how team members are talking to each other differently, even when I'm not involved. It's as if we've all come to a different level of commitment."

—Daniel

When you rebuild trust, you restore your commitment to the relationship that was hurt. When that relationship is at work, you thereby restore your commitment to your team, your organization, and your career. When you are not questioning your commitment, you can once again put your effort into the organization's mission, your team's goals, and the needs of the customers, patients, or other constituents that you serve. As Peter said, you become ready to "go to the mat" for your teammates, and you are dedicated to the organization.

This renewed outward commitment is mirrored within yourself. With confidence in who you are as a foundation, you commit to your values and seek to live by them. You are therefore much less likely to betray yourself in a way that betrays or hurts others. Your behavior at work comes across as cooperative, helpful, and respectful, and you contribute to the sense of authentic closeness that Daniel appreciates so much now.

Energy

"I have a renewed sense of respect and appreciation for Daniel. I am able to drop by his office and discuss anything—whether it is a challenging work issue, a personal matter, or the score of the last ball game. I am grateful for the connection we have and the relationship we have that is built on trust."

—Peter

"I am proud to be Peter's mentor and I am excited to be working with him. We have a special relationship that takes on energy of its own. Together we meet our goals, accomplish a lot, and have fun doing it.

—Daniel

Just as betrayal was energy-depleting, trust is energy-producing. When you rebuild trust like Daniel and Peter did in their relationship, you stop spending energy thinking about how you were hurt or hurt another. You cease to use your creative energy to think about how to get even or to blame your pain on someone else. Instead of draining your life energy by beating yourself up and second-guessing "who" you are, you use that energy to form connections, find new solutions, and help others. You are able to focus like a laser on your job and find that it invigorates you, so that you are excited to go to work. Because energy is contagious, others want to be around you, and when they are, they feel productive, too. In that place, you and your team are able to produce results like never before.

Together, the renewed confidence, commitment, and energy can transform you and your relationships. We don't use the word "transform" lightly. To us, to transform means that you remain yourself, but, because of what you have gone through ("trans"), you choose to shape your life and your perspective differently, in a different "form."

You are transformed on two linked levels: by the depth of your connection to yourself, and by the powerful connections that self-connection allows you to form with others.

Connection to Self

Through rebuilding trust, you have learned what it means to be compassionate toward yourself. You have embraced your innate humanness, and the term "self-love" takes on an entirely new meaning. You know and accept who you are, and you stop overriding your own needs and instincts because now you know that the price of doing so is too high. This sustainable presence of trust generates greater tolerance and acceptance of your whole being. You are therefore able to dissolve your defensive armor. Without the armor and blockages, you can experience more energy within yourself. You feel lighter, more focused, and more alive, as you are willing to be vulnerable around others.

Because you are more compassionate with yourself, you don't need to be right. When there is a breakdown in one of your relationships, you seek to understand it rather than to make the other person wrong. Sure, you will make mistakes and let others down. But when you do, you know how to respond. You now know which path to choose.

You are, in short, realigned with your sense of self. By being more fully aware of who you are, you expand your capacity for trust in yourself, for others—and thereby the depth of your relationships. Because you embrace the benefits that rebuilt trust offers, you find value and meaning in pain and are set up to form more enriched relationships in the future.

Connection to Others

> *"I'm not only interested in my co-workers' personal lives. I know that I need to know about their lives in order to see the whole picture and to see them as whole people."*
> —Daniel

When you choose to work through your own pain, you deepen your connection to others and create relationships in which trust is both given and received. The more self-aware you are, the more you have to give others. Because you are comfortable with your own human-ness, you give others permission to expose their own vulnerability and be human. You create and sustain the sacred space of healing in which there is the emotional and psychological safety that people will not be viewed as "less than" but instead will be accepted and supported.

Full, compassionate acceptance shifts your perspective. After you have accepted yourself as human first and employee second, you can authentically see others as humans first and co-workers second. In short, you have created a profound opportunity for the kind of con-nection that allows you to influence others, and for others to influ-ence you. You become an empathetic co-worker who others want to be around.

Transforming Others' Lives: Helping Rebuild Trust

Throughout this book, the last section of each chapter provided tips for what to do if you want to help others rebuild trust. Time and time again, our advice began with clarifying your intentions and checking to see what pain you might be carrying. The simple truth is that you cannot effectively help others when you are hurting your-self; you cannot fully support others in rebuilding trust if you have never been down that path yourself.

But if you have followed the path and experienced the transfor-mation that rebuilding trust brings, you have expanded exponen-tially your capacity to give support to others. You have learned how to provide support from the inside out. Whether you rebuilt trust because you were hurt or because you hurt another, through heal-ing you become someone who is viewed as trustworthy and someone who is there to help.

Because you are more aware, you pick up on subtle clues about what others are going through. You pay attention to the signs of confusion or doubt, and you answer lingering questions. You catch issues and offer support and reframing before there's a major break or betrayal. You are also more willing to be present and respond to the behavior that you witness. You are less likely to overlook little things that can accumulate over time to erode trust; you are more likely to pause and ask questions. By not ignoring, defending, justifying, or explaining away breaches of trust, you help to create an environment where breaches of trust become less common.

You choose to support the healing of others because you want them to have what you have discovered: *wholeness*. When others see you being both courageous and vulnerable in relationships, they feel they have permission to break out, take risks, be bold in their thinking, and honest in their emotions. With a prototype in front of them, they themselves become rigorous in practicing behaviors that build trust.

What may have started with your personal work or efforts to heal one relationship can transform your whole team into a group of people who want to work together, to grow together, to achieve and perform together. We often hear clients express this sense of possibility by saying, "Now, there is *nothing* we can't do!"

In this way, workplaces can be transformed individual by individual, relationship by relationship, and team by team. Transformation starts when one person like you discovers more fully who he is and what he has to offer. Through energy powered by individuals making and supporting the choice to rebuild trust, the pervasive culture becomes one in which people have permission and confidence to be human. The work environment becomes a place built on commitment where everyone wants to give their all—all of their heart, mind, and soul. The work environment becomes a safe and exciting place where people *want* to come to work and *want* to produce.

Rebuilding trust is not something you do just once. Healing becomes an approach to life. When things get tough, you choose to be aware and responsible. With compassion and courage as your partners, you have faith in the opportunities that rebuilding trust brings.

It may have felt to you at times that the Seven Steps for Healing took you through the uncharted waters of your emotions and experiences. It is our hope that we have supported you on your journey of self-discovery, healing, and renewal. It is our continuing hope that now you will be able to support another person or group of people on their trust rebuilding journey as well. As you encourage others to choose healing and renewal, you contribute to a world in which trust can transform not only you and your relationships, but others' lives and your workplace as well.

NOTES

Preface

1. The Seven Steps for Healing® is a registered trademark of the Reina Trust Building Institute. For ease of reading, the ® symbols have been removed from the text of this book.

Introduction

1. Trust Building® is a registered trademark of the Reina Trust Building Institute. For ease of reading, the ® symbols have been removed from the text of this book.
2. The Seven Steps for Healing® is a registered trademark of the Reina Trust Building Institute. For ease of reading, the ® symbols have been removed from the text of this book.
3. Kübler-Ross, Elisabeth. *Death: The Final Stage of Growth.* Englewood Cliffs, NJ: Prentice-Hall, 1975.

Step 2

1. Adapted from Davis, Laura. *The Courage to Heal Workbook: For Adult Survivors of Child Sexual Abuse.* New York, NY: Harper & Row, 1990.

Step 5

1. Kador, John. *Effective Apology: Mending Fences, Building Bridges, and Restoring Trust.* San Francisco: Berrett-Koehler Publishers, 2009, p. 16.

2. Dressler, Larry. *Standing in the Fire: Leading High-Heat Meetings with Calm, Clarity, and Courage*. San Francisco: Berrett-Koehler Publishers, 2010, p. xvi.

Step 6

1. Chödrön, Pema. *When Things Fall Apart: Heart Advice for Difficult Times*. Boston: Shambhala, 1997.
2. *Peaceful Warrior*. 2006. Directed by Victor Salva. Screenplay by Kevin Bernhardt. Based on the novel by Dan Millman.

ACKNOWLEDGMENTS

We talk often about the critical role of support in rebuilding trust. It is therefore with great respect and pleasure that we acknowledge the container of support that made the writing of this book and the research behind it possible.

We thank our publisher, Steve Piersanti, for saying, "Yes, this is a book whose time has come." He guided us to speak to people at all levels in the workplace. Steve, your feedback made us stronger writers. Thank you for the push and for your faith in us and in the promise of this book.

We appreciate the trust that the entire Berrett-Koehler staff has for this book and the contribution it will make. We particularly thank Kristen Frantz, vice president of sales and marketing, who has been a longtime friend, dance partner, and advisor.

Katherine Armstrong, our editor extraordinaire, provided thoughtful guidance throughout the entire development of this book. Katherine, you helped us find and honor our voice and were there every step of the way. Thank you for your support and friendship. The journey continues.

Andrea Chilcote, Rob Vaughn, Lauren Riggs, and Gauri Reyes provided invaluable feedback on the early manuscript. Thank you for your insights; they brought focus to the book.

We are grateful for the talented team at the Reina Trust Building Institute. Christopher Dilts, our trusted partner, provides a steady stream of collaboration that nurtures our creative juices.

Other dynamic associates supported us to serve our clients without skipping a beat while we worked on this book: Rob Goldberg, Chris Roland, Melodie Howard, Nancy Henjum, Chris Francovich, Elizabeth Reuthe, Lenny Diamond, Roland Livingston, Tracy Brown, and Jesse Mendoza. Heather Dieringer, our rock for the last several years, oversaw all aspects of our day-to-day operations and our trust measuring instruments while delivering the highest level of service to our clients. Norma Farnsworth provides home-base support that allows us to focus where we need to. Thank you all for your presence and for embracing our purpose to bring trust, healing, and renewal to the world.

We bring ourselves in service to our clients and are served in return. Several freely shared their stories of rebuilding trust and the lessons gained along the way so that we may share them with you. Thank you: Terri Aschul, Paul Bova, Nancy Formella, Dave Whaley, Sharon Ryan, David Williams, Thom Johnston, Randy Spencer, Davida Sharpe, Ted Mayer, Mary Beth Petersen, Denise Renter, and Sue Hoffman. Thank you for your trust in us and for the honor to support you.

We are grateful for our colleagues, Craig Runde and Tim Flanagan, who share our commitment to building and rebuilding trust in their own work. We thank them for sharing their personal stories which will make a contribution to the healing of others.

We thank Carol Mlotkowski, Sean Ryan, and Matthew Tabenken, who were so generous in giving their time and sharing their powerful stories.

Thank you, Isabelle Lambert for helping us to listen to our client's stories at a deeper level, to hear their significance, and to understand our own more deeply so that we have more to offer others.

We are grateful to the thousands of people we have had the opportunity to accompany on their healing journeys. Through your courage and compassion, we have learned the power of trust, healing, and renewal. It is through you that we felt the inspiration to write this book.

Our families continue to give encouragement and have faith in us. They have stood by us. We thank our parents, our siblings, and in-laws sprinkled across the country. Thank you for your continuing graciousness, particularly during long periods when we are not available.

Our sons, Patrick and William, and godchildren Timothy and Julia, are a source of pride and joy for us by the trustworthy way they lead their lives. They all touch our souls and inspire us to be better people. Patrick, an associate producer for reality television shows such as "The Biggest Loser," reminds us often about human nature. Timothy, a college student, and Julia, a high school student, both light up our world through their music, writing, humor, and curiousity about life. We extend special appreciation in this book to our son, Will, an Army 2nd Lieutenant platoon leader, who was courageously serving our country in Afghanistan while we developed this manuscript.

We provide special acknowledgment to Michelle's father, Jack Chagnon, to whom this book is dedicated. When, two weeks before his death, we asked if we could share elements of his story of betrayal by a fellow prisoner while in captivity by the Chinese during the Korean War, his response was, "Of course, sweetheart, anything I can do to help." Thank you, Dad. You have helped. And, as you promised, you are indeed with us each and every day. You live in our hearts forever.

INDEX

ABOUT THE AUTHORS

Photo by Kathleen Landwehrle

Dr. Dennis and Dr. Michelle Reina have devoted almost two decades of their professional lives to developing a comprehensive Trust Building® approach that helps people renew confidence, commitment, and energy in their relationships, transform cultures, and produce business results. Together and independently, they are sought-after consultants, keynote speakers, and executive coaches. Their strength lies in their proven ability to combine a rigorous, research-based foundation with a compassionate approach that recognizes the human aspect of trust. Their business-best selling first book, *Trust and Betrayal in the Workplace* won the 2007 Nautilus Book Award and the 2008 Axiom Book Award.

As co-founders of The Reina Trust Building Institute, Dennis and Michelle are thought leaders in measuring, developing, and restoring trust. The Reina Trust Building Institute offers the most comprehensive, integrated solutions to make building and rebuilding trust possible, practical and cost-effective for organizations of all kinds and of all sizes. Equally effective with Fortune 100® executives, government officials and manufacturing shift workers, Michelle, Dennis and their team customize Trust Building® solutions for individuals, small teams and expansive organizations with thousands of employees.

Dennis and Michelle each hold doctorates in human and organizational systems from Fielding Graduate University, where they met and fell in love on the dance floor. They relish their time together, hiking, canoeing, skiing, picnicking in their home state of Vermont, swimming in the Caribbean, and always dancing. Having taken their own journeys to heal from personal betrayals and significant life challenges, Michelle and Dennis feel profoundly blessed to be able to transform their own difficult experiences into daily work that helps others heal and rebuild trust. They see the people they serve as their best teachers, for their clients' experiences and courage inform their research and inspire their growth as coaches, scholarly practitioners, and writers.

WORKING WITH THE AUTHORS

Speaking

When Dennis and Michelle speak, audiences listen and respond. They take notes, engage in discussions, and sometimes shed a quiet tear. Why? Because the Reinas' material and delivery touch people in profoundly personal and emotional ways, for the topic of trust lives in people's hearts and personal experiences, not just in their minds and organizations. At the same time, Dennis and Michelle's informative, practical approach helps people learn concrete strategies that they can put into immediate action to build and rebuild trust. Dennis and Michelle are available as a team or individually for customized keynotes, conferences, and seminars anywhere in the world.

Consulting

Dennis and Michelle have devoted a combined forty years to researching and developing the Reina Trust & Betrayal Model® and a comprehensive yet practical approach to Trust Building®. The Reina Trust Building Institute partners with leaders to provide practical and measurable Trust Building® strategies and programs to integrate trust-building behaviors and methods into strategic initiatives and human performance to drive business results.

The Reina Trust Building Institute helps leaders and organizations to develop Trust-Building® strategies to drive initiatives such as employee engagement and satisfaction, change and transition, mergers and acquisitions, team and leadership development, innovation, creativity, risk taking, and collaboration. Its Trust Building® coaches use a variety of modalities, including consulting, workshops facilitated face-to-face, and/or online learning experiences that can transform cultures and produce business results.

Clients include:

American Express	Nokia
AstraZeneca	Norwich University
Ben & Jerry's	Pension Benefit Guarantee
Boeing	Sandia National Labs
Center for Creative Leadership	Standard Life
Children's Healthcare	Texas Instruments
Dartmouth-Hitchcock Medical Center	Toyota
Harvard University	U.S. Army Chaplaincy
Hewlett-Packard	U.S. Army Corps of Engineers
Johns Hopkins Medical Center	U.S. Dept. of Homeland Security
Johnson & Johnson	U.S. Treasury
Kimberly-Clark	Veterans Affairs
Kodak	Yale University
Microsoft	Wheaton Franciscan Healthcare
MillerCoors	Wyeth
Middlebury College	Walt Disney World

Trust Building® *Training Programs*

The Reina Trust Building Institute provides training programs that put the principles and Trust Building® tools discussed in this book and in *Trust and Betrayal in the Workplace* into action. The programs include core Trust Building® in the Workplace programs, executive briefings, and certification programs. Through certification, internal leaders and HR/OD professionals can acquire the knowledge and tools to measure and build trust within their own organizations.

Coaching

Dennis and Michelle provide Transformative Trust-Based Coaching®. Through a process of inquiry, reflection, and discussion, you can learn how to use the Reinas' Trust Building® and healing approach to transform your relationships and help you to be more effective at work and in life.

Trust Building® Resources

Trust Building® Measurement Tools

Dennis, Michelle, and their Reina Trust Building Institute team have developed research-based, statistically valid, and reliable web-based tools to measure trust and benchmark your Trust Building® progress at the organization, team, individual, leader, customer, and patient levels. These tools provide data and insight that inform Trust Building® programs and produce results.

Trust Building® Online

This powerful community-building tool creates a 24/7 asynchronous (not-at-the-same-time), self-paced or facilitator-led, web-based learning environment that supports sustainable Trust Building® and drives desired business outcomes.

Desktop Guides and Wall Charts

Desktop quick-reference guides and wall charts of the Seven Steps for Healing® and the Reina Trust & Betrayal Model® are available for purchase at www.ReinaTrustBuilding.com. They are great tools to maintain awareness, support discussion, and practice of trust building behaviors.

Contact Information

The Reina Trust Building Institute
560 Black Bear Run
Stowe, VT 05672
Phone: 802-253-8808
Email: info@reinatrustbuilding.com
www.ReinaTrustBuilding.com

Also by Dennis and Michelle Reina

Trust and Betrayal in the Workplace
Building Effective Relationships in Your Organization
Second Edition, Revised and Expanded

Dennis and Michelle Reina's award-winning, landmark first book lays the groundwork for *Rebuilding Trust in the Workplace*. *Trust and Betrayal in the Workplace* tells you everything you need to know about trust: the power unleashed when it exists, the problems created when it doesn't, and the pain suffered when it is betrayed. Through in-depth, practical guidelines it clearly explains the dynamics of trust and helps organization members develop a common language to discuss trust-related issues, to identify behaviors that build and break trust, and to take action to improve performance and boost bottom-line results through trust building.

Paperback, 272 pages, ISBN 978-1-57675-377-4
PDF ebook, ISBN 978-1-57675-949-3

Berrett–Koehler Publishers, Inc.
www.bkconnection.com

800.929.2929

Berrett–Koehler
Publishers

Berrett-Koehler is an independent publisher dedicated to an ambitious mission: *Creating a World That Works for All*.

We believe that to truly create a better world, action is needed at all levels—individual, organizational, and societal. At the individual level, our publications help people align their lives with their values and with their aspirations for a better world. At the organizational level, our publications promote progressive leadership and management practices, socially responsible approaches to business, and humane and effective organizations. At the societal level, our publications advance social and economic justice, shared prosperity, sustainability, and new solutions to national and global issues.

A major theme of our publications is "Opening Up New Space." Berrett-Koehler titles challenge conventional thinking, introduce new ideas, and foster positive change. Their common quest is changing the underlying beliefs, mindsets, institutions, and structures that keep generating the same cycles of problems, no matter who our leaders are or what improvement programs we adopt.

We strive to practice what we preach—to operate our publishing company in line with the ideas in our books. At the core of our approach is stewardship, which we define as a deep sense of responsibility to administer the company for the benefit of all of our "stakeholder" groups: authors, customers, employees, investors, service providers, and the communities and environment around us.

We are grateful to the thousands of readers, authors, and other friends of the company who consider themselves to be part of the "BK Community." We hope that you, too, will join us in our mission.

A BK Business Book

This book is part of our BK Business series. BK Business titles pioneer new and progressive leadership and management practices in all types of public, private, and nonprofit organizations. They promote socially responsible approaches to business, innovative organizational change methods, and more humane and effective organizations.

Berrett–Koehler
Publishers

A community dedicated to creating
a world that works for all

Visit Our Website: www.bkconnection.com

Read book excerpts, see author videos and Internet movies, read our
authors' blogs, join discussion groups, download book apps, find out about
the BK Affiliate Network, browse subject-area libraries of books, get special
discounts, and more!

Subscribe to Our Free E-Newsletter, the *BK Communiqué*

Be the first to hear about new publications, special discount offers, exclu-
sive articles, news about bestsellers, and more! Get on the list for our free
e-newsletter by going to **www.bkconnection.com**.

Get Quantity Discounts

Berrett-Koehler books are available at quantity discounts for orders of ten or
more copies. Please call us toll-free at (800) 929-2929 or email us at **bkp
.orders@aidcvt.com**.

Join the BK Community

BKcommunity.com is a virtual meeting place where people from around
the world can engage with kindred spirits to create a world that works for
all. **BKcommunity.com** members may create their own profiles, blog, start
and participate in forums and discussion groups, post photos and videos,
answer surveys, announce and register for upcoming events, and chat with
others online in real time. Please join the conversation!